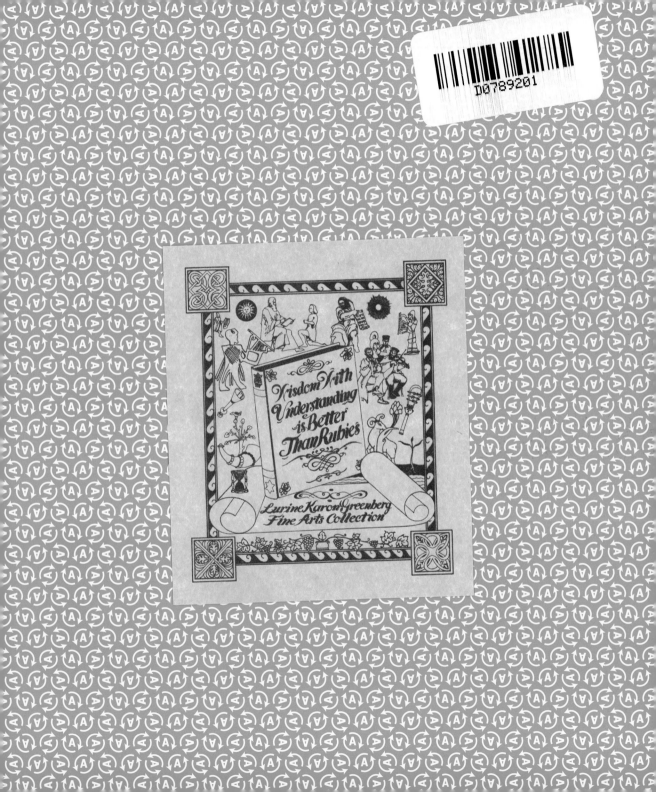

Wisdom With
Understanding
is Better
Than Rubies

Lurine Karon Greenberg
Fine Arts Collection

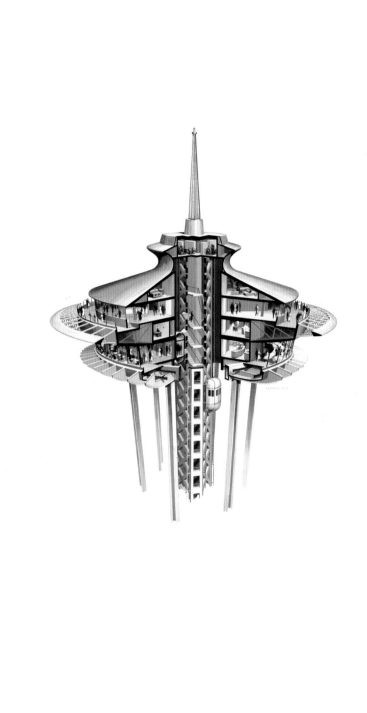

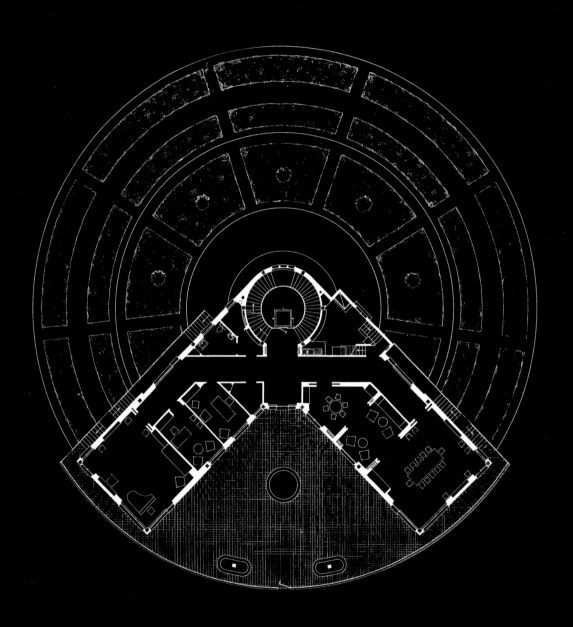

REVOLVING
ARCHITECTURE
A HISTORY OF BUILDINGS THAT ROTATE, SWIVEL, AND PIVOT

CHAD RANDL

PRINCETON ARCHITECTURAL PRESS
NEW YORK

To Mom & Dad

—

PUBLISHED BY
Princeton Architectural Press, 37 East 7th Street, New York, NY 10003
For a free catalog of books, call 1.800.722.6657 Visit our web site at www.papress.com

This book has been supported by a grant from the Graham Foundation for Advanced Studies in the Fine Arts.
The Space Needle is a registered trademark of Space Needle LLC and is used with permission.

EDITING Dorothy Ball   DESIGN Paul Wagner

SPECIAL THANKS TO
Nettie Aljian, Sara Bader, Nicola Bednarek, Janet Behning, Becca Casbon, Penny (Yuen Pik) Chu,
Russell Fernandez, Pete Fitzpatrick, Wendy Fuller, Jan Haux, Clare Jacobson,
John King, Aileen Kwun, Nancy Eklund Later, Linda Lee, Laurie Manfra, Katharine Myers,
Lauren Nelson Packard, Jennifer Thompson, Arnoud Verhaeghe, Joseph Weston, and Deb Wood of
Princeton Architectural Press —Kevin C. Lippert, publisher

LIBRARY OF CONGRESS CATALOGING-IN-PUBLICATION DATA
Randl, Chad.
Revolving architecture : a history of buildings that rotate, swivel, and pivot / Chad Randl.
p.   cm.
Includes bibliographical references and index.
ISBN 978-1-56898-681-4 (alk. paper)
1. Revolving buildings. I. Title.
NA8490.R36 2008
721—DC22   2007047378

CONTENTS

ACKNOWLEDGMENTS

The kindness of friends and colleagues, many of whom were strangers a few years ago, made this book possible. They received phone calls, letters, and emails and responded generously with insights, anecdotes, suggestions, corrections, photographs, brochures, postcards, drawings, and leads for finding more of the same. They hosted me at their offices, and rotating homes, and restaurants, (and jail), and let me push the button or turn the crank to put the building in motion. I am especially grateful to Lidia Invernizzi, Lorella Campi Gandini, Professor Aurelio Galfetti, Simone Nicolini, Luigi Colani, Martin Brümmerhoff, Uwe Schmidt, Annette Müller, Rolf Disch, Boris Kauth, Eric and Marc Halter, Tamara Hemmerlein, Al and Janet Johnstone, Bill Butler, Don Dunick, Christian Lintl, Clarence Reed, Margaret Campbell, Ron Miller, John Portman, Anthony Rubano, Patrick Stacey, Gregory Donofrio, Irene Thali, Boo Pergament, Luke Everingham, Debra Gust, Bing Xu, and Nancy Noonan. Portions of this book were presented at a Society of Architectural Historians conference session on kinetic architecture. I would like to thank the session chair Victoria Young and presenters, Nicole Watson, Taiji Miyasaka, and Eran Neuman for their fruitful discussions about this topic. Aviva Zuk Share, and the family of William Zuk, provided financial assistance for the session. At Princeton Architectural Press, Kevin Lippert and Jennifer Thompson recognized the significance of rotating architecture and provided early encouragement. The manuscript benefited immensely from Dorothy Ball's thoughtful review and editorial guidance. Paul Wagner's admirable design skills translated the subject's dynamism to the printed page. The Graham Foundation for Advanced Studies in the Fine Arts provided essential support for the research and production of this book. Final thanks go to Melissa and the girls for their patience and support.

INTRODUCTION

In 1906 American newspaper columnist George Ade described planning a transatlantic voyage and reserving a stateroom that he assumed would be filled with sunlight and warm breezes throughout the crossing. At the outset of the journey, however, he was disappointed to realize that the ship had to turn around as it left the dock, and that his cabin would actually face north "with nothing coming in at the porthole except a current of cold air direct from Labrador." The experience gave him an idea:

> The unexpected manner in which the boat turned around has suggested to me a scheme for a revolving apartment house. The building will be set on giant casters and will revolve slowly, so that every apartment will have a southern exposure at certain hours of the day, to say nothing of the advantage of getting a new view every few minutes. It is well known that apartments with southern exposure and overlooking the Boulevard command a double rental. When every apartment may have a southern exposure and face the main thoroughfare, think of the tremendous increase in revenues![1]

Ade was not the first to come up with the idea of a rotating building, but his description and his plans to capitalize upon it neatly typify the development of rotating architecture throughout the twentieth century. With ever-changing vantage points revolving buildings offered a new way of looking at the world. They rewrote spatial relationships within buildings and reconfigured views of the world outside. With gears, motors, and ball bearings they made nature serve the occupant, for climate or lighting control, entertainment or spectacle. Amateur inventors, entrepreneurs, and eccentrics took up the challenge of designing a viable, affordable version for their own use or to package and sell to the public. Like George Ade's epiphany many of these designs were never built, but remained elusive visions of a revolving future.

The wheel was probably the earliest rotating tool, and since its introduction history has seen innumerable adaptations. From ancient waterwheels and medieval windmills to the winches, gears, and pulleys Leonardo da Vinci drew in his notebooks, rotating devices overcame the limitations of human muscle and multiplied available power and space. Early engineers placed derricks, pile drivers, and excavating and dredging cranes on turntables to increase their range and facilitate movement. In time other rotating buildings appeared that were constructed for a variety of pragmatic and otherworldly reasons.

Revolving structures referenced the rotation of the earth and the annular movements of the heavens; they could remain in synchrony with the sun throughout the day and follow the stars at night. Legendary palace halls with rotating domes made to resemble the nighttime sky suggest a human fascination with the mysteries of the universe and a consideration of the place of humans within it. The first observatory with a rotating telescope and dome was constructed in Kassel, Germany, in the sixteenth century. Space stations planned in the twentieth century would rotate to simulate gravity in outer space.

Like technology in general, rotating structures facilitated destruction and creation; some were deadly serious, others were for play. Rotating devices raised siege engines and aimed large cannon and their armored enclosures toward an approaching threat. Rotating altars divided into three sections, like that built in the New York City Women's House of Detention in 1933, allowed a single interior space to be readily adapted for Protestant, Catholic, and Jewish religious services.[2] Revolving stages helped entertain theater audiences by enabling quick scenery changes and new forms of dynamic staging. At a time when cameras and film stock were not sensitive, early motion pictures were filmed in three-walled roofless rooms that could be rotated to maintain optimal natural light and position shadows. Spinning amusement rides and steel towers with turning arms and wheels thrilled fairgoers and seaside vacationers.

From at least the Middle Ages structures meant to be lived in—for short visits or during a meal—were made to turn. Detached dining halls and gazebo-like shelters located in the pleasure gardens of the European nobility impressed visitors and provided variable vistas of surrounding landscapes. In the 1800s writers first imagined a future of revolving residences. At the dawn of the next century, fueled by new technological developments and an atmosphere of can-do ingenuity, a diverse group of entrepreneurs, architects, amateur builders, physicians, and health advocates sought to realize the dream of a rotating house.

Designers were drawn to the concept for many reasons. The range of structures, forms, and mechanisms they came up with reflected their various motives and the cultural atmosphere in which they worked. Some maximized living space in apartments and houses by incorporating partitioned turntables—at the turn of a crank or the flip of a switch, a living room became a bedroom. Rotating houses that turned in their entirety could be swung into or out of breezes and the sun's rays to regulate the effects of outside conditions upon the building interior. Sanatoriums in the early 1900s used rotating cottages to keep tuberculosis patients bathed in daylight. The view out the windows of externally rotating houses could be altered at the occupant's whim, overturning the static relationship between building and site that had essentially remained unchanged since the beginning of architecture.

In the first half of the twentieth century rotating bars appeared in highbrow hotels and nightclubs. Patrons enjoyed cocktails as their stools and bar top slowly orbited a central core of bartenders and bottles. In the post–World War II era entrepreneurs and architects combined this concept with rooftop dining and new tower construction to inaugurate an era of revolving restaurants. Dinner at a table in a room slowly revolving high in the air became a tourist's ritual and a favored setting for anniversaries and special events. Cities around the world raced to build revolving restaurants on top of hotels, office buildings, and communication towers, seeing them as symbols of modernity and progress.

Ostensibly the revolving structures that developed over time appear to have little in common. The reasons for rotating a windmill seem very different from the reason that restaurants were rotated in the postwar era. Stages were turned for entertainment, while treatment shelters were turned in grave efforts to cure respiratory diseases. The mechanics of rotation also varied considerably. Some were turned by hand, others with hydraulic pressure or motors powered by solar panels; some only turned half circles, while others could rotate 360 degrees without limit. Angelo Invernizzi's 1936 revolving house near Verona, Italy, took over nine hours to make a complete revolution while the restaurant in London's 1965 Post Office Tower revolved every twenty-two minutes.

Yet despite their differences, revolving structures across time, geography, and function shared many similarities. Revolving architecture was a product of inquisitive problem-solvers determined to improve existing ways of working, living, and thinking. Many of the buildings and designs reflect a belief in the beneficence of technology, that

the right machine could solve almost any problem, that the new way was the better way. In some cases designers let their ideas and passion for mechanical solutions outweigh all else—the occupants' comfort and convenience was secondary to the rotating feature. This faith in technology as a means of progress often mirrored broader cultural perspectives. But there were also signs that the public viewed revolving designs with some ambivalence.

Over the past hundred and thirty years, newspaper and magazine stories, a Broadway farce, novels, movies, and television programs have depicted rotating buildings. In most the designs are met with curiosity tempered by a wariness of their future implications. Rotating houses were lauded by health officials for maximizing the salutary effects of sunlight and ventilation, but were lampooned in essays and editorials as proof that society had run amuck. Rotating buildings were dismissed by the architectural establishment as little more than follies at the same time many assumed them to be inevitable designs of the future. Attendees at world's fairs and home shows lined up to see the latest rotating kitchen, but few wanted one in their own house.

Revolving restaurants and the vertiginous towers that supported them were especially tempting subjects for ridicule. East Berlin's TV tower with its revolving "Telecafe" was called the "Tele-Asparagus." London's Post Office Tower, which transmitted telephone signals and housed a revolving restaurant near the top, was referred to as "a modern Tower of Babel." Food critics found a correlation between the price of the entrees and the height of the restaurant. Humorist Calvin Trillin once wrote, "I never eat in a restaurant that's over a hundred feet off the ground and won't stand still."[3]

* * *

As far back as ancient Rome, rotating architecture has been a symbol of conspicuous consumption, a showpiece for the well-to-do. Rotating designs were meant to awe or at least impress. Automobile turntables set in driveways and private garages seemed as essential as chauffeurs to wealthy motorists of the early twentieth century. Any bachelor pad of 1960s and '70s worthy of the name had a revolving bed to signal sexual prowess and economic success. In Don DeLillo's 2003 novel *Cosmopolis*, the main character, a young, single, billionaire trader, battles insomnia reading poetry in his rotating bedroom atop a Manhattan skyscraper.[4]

Rotating structures were not unusual only because they could turn. Their physical forms were often shaped to maximize the effect of their ability to turn. Many also reflected the individualistic aesthetics of designers dissatisfied with conventional architecture. As a result revolving houses, restaurants, hotels, and other structures frequently bore little resemblance to past buildings. Perched on pedestals, dome shaped, hexagonal, with faceted wall planes and unusual glazing configurations, the range of unorthodox design decisions seems to further distance rotating structures from other buildings.

Examined in isolation or even as a group, it is tempting to consider rotating structures simply as architectural freaks, standing outside established narratives of the past. But they have counterparts. In their ability to move, revolving architecture can be placed within the general category of kinetic design. Identified and explored by William Zuk and Roger H. Clark in their 1970 book *Kinetic Architecture*, buildings of this type are by definition adaptable to changing environmental conditions and programmatic needs.[5] They use barometers, photoelectric cells, and anemometers to evaluate conditions and engage motors to extend, retract, fold, unfold, or turn automatically. The form or orientation of these designs can respond to the time of day, position of the sun, cloud cover, and existence of wind or precipitation. Movement in kinetic designs can also be initiated manually based on the weather, the occupants' activities, their desire for greater privacy or openness, or pure whim.

Zuk and Clark discuss auditoriums and stadiums with moveable seating and retractable roofs, self-erecting shelters, pneumatic exhibition pavilions, revolving structures, and a variety of experimental and conceptual designs for modular buildings and cities intended to be expanded incrementally. They argue that movement is change and that architecture needs to change—both individual structures reorientable from one moment to the next, and the field of design adapting to new ideas of what buildings should be capable of doing. Rotating designs strive to achieve this vital flexibility.

Dismissing rotating structures as quirky and exceptional diminishes the lessons that can be derived from them. An exploration of these buildings reveals the reasons why architects, engineers, entrepreneurs, and owners wanted their houses, restaurants, jails, theaters, and other structures to turn. But it also reveals valuable insights into how structures are viewed and perceived by the public, how designers reach decisions about how to best articulate their personal visions, and how themes in popular culture—the turn-of-the-twentieth-century obsession with efficiency, the post–World War II fascination with space travel—leave marks on our built landscape.

While this study is an architectural investigation of buildings that turn, it also looks at the cultural atmosphere that gave rise to the concept in various locations at various times. Rotating buildings are cultural artifacts. As such, they provide insights into the people that constructed them, their concerns, hopes, interests, and view of the world around them. Even buildings that were planned but never constructed, envisioned but never realized, tell us about their designers and the eras in which they lived. In the first half of the twentieth century revolving structures were "mechanical contrivances" well suited to the machine age. Revolving designs reflected the kinetic energy of a period increasingly characterized by motion and movement, electric motors, trains, cars, and the beginnings of aviation. During the post–World War II era revolving architecture was a product of the space age, transistors, and circuits, and, later, innovations in smart and green design.

The story of the rotating building is entwined with the stories of mechanization and the assumed impending victory of automation. The machine's impact on our environment, on work, and on life in general has been well documented. One seminal work is Wolfgang Schivelbusch's book on the transformative effect of an older, much more pervasive artifact, the railway: *The Railway Journey: The Industrialization and Perception of Time and Space*.[6] In the foreword Alan Trachtenberg notes that cultural historians have looked for "new forms of consciousness arising out of new structures, new things. One feature of modernity as it crystallized in the 19th century was a radical foregrounding of machinery and mechanical apparatus within everyday life." Trachtenberg advocates a search "for evidence of culture at those minute points of contact between new things and old habits, and that we include in our sense of history the power of things themselves to impress and shape and evoke a response within consciousness."[7]

Throughout their history, rotating buildings have been heralded as architecture of the future and their imminent adoption widely anticipated. But that anticipation continues. The dream of a viable, popularly accepted, and affordable rotating residence remains elusive. Other forms have come and gone. Examples of built designs, designs that went nowhere, the motives, influences, and approaches of their developers, the continuing popular curiosity about rotating homes, the appearance of the rotary jail, the rotating tower, the revolving stage, and the revolving restaurant show new, mechanical things contacting old habits. They deserve a closer look.

CHAPTER ONE

EARLY HISTORY OF ROTATING BUILDINGS

In AD 64 a devastating fire swept through the capital of the Roman Empire, leaving swaths of the city center smoldering and uninhabitable. Emperor Nero took this opportunity to build a vast, luxurious residence and landscaped parkland called the Domus Aurea, or Golden House. Later, Nero's critics found several features of the palace symbolic of his megalomaniacal self-indulgence, including its artificial lake, the 100-foot-tall statue of the emperor, and rooms with revolving mechanisms. According to Suetonius, writing some sixty years after Nero's death, there were several spaces that rotated: "the supper rooms were vaulted, and compartments of the ceilings, inlaid with ivory, were made to revolve, and scatter flowers; while they contained pipes which shed unguents upon the guests. The chief banqueting room was circular, and revolved perpetually, night and day, in imitation of the motion of the celestial bodies."[1]

But scholars have yet to determine definitively what Suetonius was talking about. When a large octagonal hall was discovered in one of the Domus Aurea's surviving wings, it was declared a likely candidate for the legendary rotating dining hall. This vaulted room surely was a showcase space with a grand interior and domed ceiling. Because nothing in the room suggests the former presence

of rotating apparatus, some have suggested that the dome's wide oculus was covered by a lantern with constellations illustrated on its underside, and that this lantern rotated on wheels or rollers set in a grooved track.[2] Others have speculated that the rotating dining room was a detached, probably wood-framed, merry-go-round-like structure located elsewhere on the palace grounds.[3] A final theory is that Suetonius was simply exaggerating the effect of the sun's passage though the oculus while reinforcing the emperor's reputation as a grandiose despot.

However it functioned, and whether it even existed, the concept of Nero's rotating dining hall remains a powerful symbol of revolving architecture and how such architecture was presented and perceived. Clearly Suetonius's story is meant to show the design as the work of one determined to dazzle his visitors. It suggested that Nero claimed power extending even to control of the earth and the heavens. It conflated rotation and illusion and suggested an effort to fool the senses. The rotating dome placed the owner at the center of the universe, increasing his prestige and perceived status in relation to all others. This centric attitude, in which occupants appeared stationary as the world turned around them, was a perception promoted by many of the rotating houses and other structures that followed.

In the centuries after Nero, royalty from other lands made similar use of the spectacle of moving architecture. Byzantine and later medieval sources describe a temple or palace erected by the Persian king Chosroes in the seventh century AD. Its domed ceiling featured representations of constellations and the interior simulated rain and thunder. In the center a throne or statue sat atop a column that was rotated by means of draft animals in the room below. Three hundred years later, the caliph of Cordoba, Abd ar-Rahman III (also known as an-Nasir), constructed a dramatic audience hall in his palace. A chronicler described the domed room as having walls encrusted with jewels, gold, and silver that were made to rotate. Some accounts describe this motion as an illusion produced by an enormous pool of mercury located in the center of the room:

> Whenever an-Nasir wished to awe a man present in his…company, he would signal one of his Slav slaves to put in motion that quicksilver, thereby light would be produced like lightning flashes which would arrest the hearts of those assembled, until it would appear to all…as long as the quicksilver was in motion, that the place was rotating about them. It was said that this *majlis* [audience hall] circled and oriented itself toward the sun.[4]

Rotation for Early Industry

Rotation was also used in a less theatrical manner to save energy and lighten labors. The wheel's discovery and first utilization is beyond the recorded past, but subsequent applications of wheeled tools can be more easily identified. By placing a flat stone disk on a pivot and turning it by hand, potters, as early as 3000 BC, dramatically increased the speed and precision of their work shaping clay. According to historians of technology, the mechanical revolution and reliance upon the machine can be traced back to this modest invention, "the momentum of the spinning wheel, which reduces the muscular effort on the part of the potter to almost nothing, gave man one of the first of the long series of labor-saving devices out of which modern industry has developed."[5]

In the centuries that followed, basic pulleys, winches, gears, and screws maximized the power of human and animal muscle. From ancient Rome to the Arab Empire to India and China, these wheels were combined into increasingly complicated mechanisms for increasingly diverse functions. Pumps, screw presses, spinning wheels, mechanical clocks, and cranes all relied on rotating elements.

Watermills were among the first machines that captured the effortless energy of nature—to mill grain and operate saws, bellows, and forge hammers. Where there was no ready source of flowing water, millers adapted the technology to take advantage of wind power. Though their exact provenance is unknown, it is believed that windmills initially appeared in England, France, or Flanders beginning in the twelfth century. They spread along the coast of northern Europe to Scandinavia and Russia before the Crusades brought them to the Middle East.

These first windmills were called post mills as the main enclosed structure (called a buck) sat upon and rotated around a central

wood post. The buck contained the gears and shafts that used the rotation of the enormous sweeps to turn the millstone or pump water. The post was made of a single tree trunk measuring up to two feet in diameter. Below the buck a wood or masonry roundhouse usually enclosed the post and support framing. Steps extended from the buck to the ground on the side opposite the sweeps, as did a long beam called a tail pole. To prevent the sweeps hitting cattle, mills were occasionally ringed by a ditch.[6]

Though exponentially more efficient than the hand querns and horse mills they replaced, post mills were still labor intensive and potentially dangerous machines. When the wind shifted direction, the mill had to be turned to face it. To rotate the buck the miller would lift the ladder off the ground, grasp the tailpole, and wrench the entire structure into position. Some mills were turned using rope and windlasses anchored to posts surrounding the mill. Like giant weathervanes, later versions were made to rotate into the wind automatically by a fantail attached to the tailpole.

During a storm the speed of the sweeps could be moderated by turning them out of

Illustration of post mills in Belgium, from the sixteenth-century book *Nova Reperta* by Johannes Stradanus

Post mills in Siberia, Russia, 1912

the wind or by means of an internal brake (which risked generating excessive heat and starting a fire). On early versions with wood-frame sweeps, the miller could roll up a portion of the fabric cover, reducing the area exposed to the wind. Later improvements included shuttered sweeps with springs that would open to spill excess wind, slowing the rotation. Eventually fittings were developed that allowed the miller to control the shutters while the mill was in motion.

An exceptionally long-lived technology, post mills remained in operation around the world well into the second half of the twentieth century. Their development had a profound impact upon local economies, the cost of bread, and population growth.

They furthered technological innovation and threatened the established social order (some early post mills were developed by entrepreneurs looking to escape the feudal system, where local lords and abbots monopolized grain milling and therefore controlled prices). Turned in response to changing weather conditions, post mills are an early example of architecture made instantly adaptable to the world outside.

Rotating Engineering and Architecture in the Renaissance

During the Renaissance drawings of toothed wheels, pin-gear wheels, screws, shafts, and axles, as well as the mechanisms and structures they made possible, populated the writings of numerous artist-engineers. Leonardo da Vinci sketched the rotating cranes that Filippo Brunelleschi invented to meet the unprecedented challenges of constructing the Basilica di Santa Maria del Fiore. His own designs included an antifriction bearing and an epicyclic gear assembly, with a small gear that rotated within the circumference of a larger gear. Though the applications of these mechanisms are not described, the former is a clear antecedent to the modern ball bearing track, or "race" used in some rotating designs to the present day. Agostino Ramelli used an epicyclic gear for his 1588 revolving reading desk, perhaps influenced by Leonardo's drawings.[7] The device illustrated an efficient means of displaying open books in a limited space—only the text needed at the moment was at the forefront, while the remaining books were out of sight but readily accessible. Such revolving furniture was an important antecedent to later internally rotating house designs.

Renaissance innovations in engineering were accompanied by a flowering of building design and theory. Architectural literature authored during the period included important treatises by Leon Battista Alberti, Andrea Palladio, Sebastiano Serlio, and Vincenzo Scamozzi. Architectural writers drew links between contemporary design practices and those of the classical past, attempted to define and codify appropriate proportions, and proposed ideal building forms for future development.

The latter was the case with a building that architect and sculptor Antonio di Pietro Averlino, better know as Filarete, included in his 1462 *Treatise on Architecture*. In the work,

Filarete presented his ideas about design through the story of a model city called Sforzinda and its mythical port, Plusiapolis. The project is described in a narrative dialogue with the story's architect (a thinly disguised Filarete) explaining its various buildings to his patrons (modeled after the author's own benefactors, the Sforza family). Toward the end of the book, Filarete describes a revolving tower made of stone. The rectangular base of the tower was twenty

Agostino Ramelli's rotary reading desk, 1588

braccia (a unit of measurement equivalent to the length of an arm) high with arched entrances on each facade. Above, a five-story shaft with columns shaped like human figures rotated on an enormous ball socket set in the base bushing. The tower was crowned with a statue depicting the son of Milan's real-life regent, Galeazzo Sforza, on a rearing horse.[8] Filarete did not elaborate on the tower's function. Its role appears to have been primarily monumental.

Towers have long symbolized technological accomplishment, civic pride, and political authority. Icons—whether statues of post–Soviet era megalomaniacs or restaurants placed atop towers—emphasize control over technology and the land below. By placing a likeness of the leader's son on the structure and by making it turn, Filarete demonstrated his own flair as a designer, flattered his patron, and asserted that patron's domination. Indeed, rotation heightened the allusion to Sforza's power; a statue that turned was all-seeing and all-knowing. Like twentieth-century planners redeveloping city centers, Filarete may have also recognized the need for an attention-getting tower to serve as a focal point for this new vision of urban life.

Rotation for Defense—Towers and Turrets
Renaissance design, like technical innovation in general, was often driven by military necessity. Throughout history fighting forces have sought advantage with stronger swords, thicker walls, and quieter submarines. Advances in metal and casting technology created powerful artillery that rendered obsolete existing fortifications, rotary machine

Detail of page from Filarete's *Treatise on Architecture* showing his rotating tower, ca. 1462

tooling enabled more accurate rifled gun barrels, and machine guns exponentially multiplied firing rates. Great strides in the mechanization of war were made during the nineteenth century. At least two designs were proposed (but ultimately never built) in the first decades for floating rotating batteries meant to protect ports and harbors from invasion by sea. With multiple cannon facing outward like spokes on a wheel, these circular batteries had platforms that turned to aim each gun at the target so that they could be fired in rapid succession.[9]

In 1841, Theodore Timby, a nineteen-year-old from Syracuse, New York, came up with his own design for a land-based revolving gun tower.[10] To illustrate the invention he carved a miniature version from a four-inch block of ivory. The following year he built an ironclad model seven feet in diameter, and in January 1843 he patented the idea. Timby must have been a persuasive talker and impressive model builder, for later that summer he demonstrated the model for President John Tyler at New York's City Hall.

The full-scale version was to be a two-story cast-iron cylinder one hundred feet in diameter set on a masonry foundation with an inner and outer ring and an elaborate mechanism for targeting and firing. Each of the outer ring's two tiers housed thirty guns firing through staggered portholes along the exterior wall. Powered by a 250-horsepower steam engine, the ring was designed to rotate once a minute upon a series of friction rollers. The inner core, which turned independently of the perimeter ring, had a dome-shaped control center rising above the outer ring's crenellated parapet. Here, the

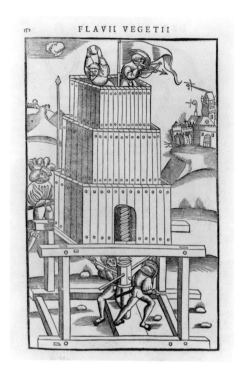

FLAVII VEGETII

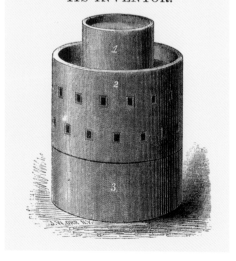

THE REVOLVING TOWER AND ITS INVENTOR.

TOP: Telescoping siege machine from an Italian book on military technology published in 1532
RIGHT: Timby's model for his revolving tower

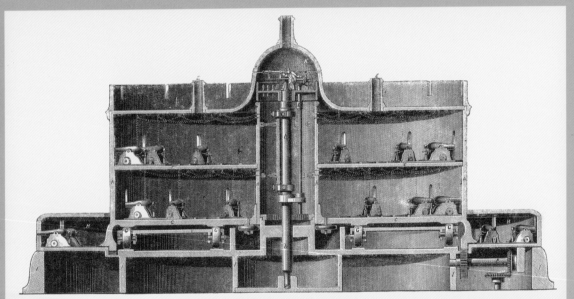

VERTICAL SECTION OF REVOLVING TOWER.

commander rotated (by hand crank) the inner turret until his telescope lined up with a targeted ship. The outer ring was then set in motion, and, as each gun turned past the precise position of the telescope, an electrical connection was tripped that fired the guns in succession. The crew below had only to reload and raise or lower the guns to set their range. Through this system, the central core would have functioned like a submarine's periscope-equipped conning tower, and each cannon in the outer ring, like the individual barrels of a Gatling gun.

Over a twenty-year period, Timby constructed at least five different scale models of his rotating tower. Newspapers and magazines including *Scientific American* and *Harper's* published articles about the design. He tirelessly demonstrated the various models before the general public and a long list of politicians and military leaders—New England governors, cabinet officials, members of Congress, officers of the Army and Navy, and French authorities in Paris. Despite these efforts he was unable to convince anyone to pay for a full-sized operable one. It took the outbreak of the American Civil War in 1861 for a pared-down and portable version of the rotating turret to find its way into battle—aboard a new type of warship.

The USS *Monitor* was made entirely of iron. Its low profile, sitting just two feet above the water line, was interrupted only by the pilothouse and a large circular turret with a pair of openings for the cannon. (One Confederate sailor likened its profile to "an immense shingle floating on the water with a gigantic cheese box rising from its centre."[11]) Powered by two steam engines,

the turret rotated a full 360 degrees. The vessel's inventor, Swedish-born John Ericsson, claimed the *Monitor* was based upon an earlier turreted ship design he had presented to the emperor of France in 1854. However, before the *Monitor* was put to sea, Theodore Timby called upon Ericsson's financial backers, noted his past work on the revolving tower, and was eventually granted a cash payment for his unwitting contribution to the project.

Shortly after it was commissioned in 1862, the *Monitor* fought a Confederate ironclad, CSS *Virginia*, to a draw in the Battle of Hampton Roads. The importance of this engagement to the future of naval warfare and warship design was immediately recognized—older wood ships and fixed cannon were no match for iron plating and rotating turrets. Before the end of the war, the US Navy had more than fifty *Monitor*-type vessels. Over the next two decades, improved and enlarged rotating armaments became standard features of warships and revolutionized the tactics of fighting at sea.[12]

Land-based multi-gun revolving towers of the type Theodore Timby envisioned were never developed. However, there were cases where less-elaborate armored rotating turret emplacements with large-caliber guns were constructed on land, usually on coasts and borders susceptible to invasion. Revolving turrets were an important element of the Maginot Line, a string of fortified bunkers, casemates, and anti-tank barriers the French military built along the German border before World War II. Each turret featured paired machine guns, howitzers, or mortars. Set in protective steel-and-

Retracted rotating turret at Schoenenbourg Fortress, Maginot Line, France, 2006

concrete shells several feet thick, the turrets were raised, lowered, and rotated 360 degrees using electric motors. In the 1940s the German Navy defended stretches of its occupied coastline using steel turrets scavenged from decommissioned ships and captured enemy vessels.[13]

Follies in the Garden—Revolving Summer Houses

Since at least the twelfth century, summer houses have been a common feature of the gardens and parks enjoyed by European nobility.[14] Count Robert II of Artois established the park of Hesdin in northern France in 1295. Within its walls the enormous garden had orchards, fish ponds, pools and fountains, vineyards, meadows, forests, and marshland. To complement these natural features, Robert of Artois constructed a variety of ornamental structures including a menagerie, an aviary, a chapel, and a large banqueting pavilion. Philip the Good, Robert's successor, added other structures, including what one historian described as "a dining house on wheels that could be rolled out to the park and turned to face the sun."[15] Such a structure took Nero's rotating dining room one step further, making it entirely mobile.

A 1736 illustration of London's Kensington Gardens by Bernard Lens the Younger shows what is described in the title as a "revolving summer house." Lens was best known as a painter of miniatures—small portraits used as mementos, calling cards, and jewelry. Like a small-scale Parthenon on the Acropolis, the summer house sat atop a mount overlooking the palace garden. Royal Gardener Charles Bridgeman had recently reworked the site, introducing asymmetrical,

*Revolving Summer House and Mount
at Kensington Gardens* by Bernard
Lens the Younger, 1736

irregular features to the previously formal and geometric landscape. Winding paths, lawns, and tree-lined avenues offered opportunities to experience and meditate on a landscape that was handcrafted to appear naturalistic. In fact, the mount itself was man-made from earth excavated to create a pond elsewhere on the grounds. To facilitate viewing the site and to provide locations for contemplation, Bridgeman and his contemporaries introduced shelters, fake ruins, and summer houses as vantage points in the landscape.

William Kent, a painter, architect, furniture designer, landscape architect, and Bridgeman's successor as royal gardener, designed the summer house depicted in Lens's illustration in 1733.[16] It resembled a small temple with an arched opening on the front flanked by caryatids supporting a simple pediment. Its function as both an object to see and a platform to see from is confirmed by Lens's composition. The house is in the center of the picture. Park goers on the ground can admire the house on the mount while above, others observe the landscape spreading out beneath them. By rotating the structure, visitors could presumably change at will the perspective framed by the house's opening. At the same time, they altered how the little house was seen from below.

The presence of a revolving garden house and dining halls in such prominent sites indicates that such buildings could be respectable features of designed landscapes. But references to other revolving structures beginning in the seventeenth century suggest they were also found in more humble settings. English political theorist James Harrington wrote

his most famous tract, *The Commonwealth of Oceana* (1656), in a revolving summer house that he turned on its pivot to face the sun. Harrington's mental health later degenerated, and, sequestered in the house, he suffered visions that included his thoughts turning into flies and bees that swarmed around his head as he wrote.[17] It is not known whether rotation aggravated or soothed the author's disorder.

In 1900 a magazine called *Living Age* published a long essay entitled "The Elders of Arcady" by English minister and schoolmaster Augustus Jessopp.[18] In this rumination on aging, memory, and earlier generations, Jessopp recounts the lives, stories, and eccentricities of several elderly persons, most of whom had lived in his village, Scarning, west of Norwich. One named Brightmore Trollop, a successful woodworker living in the 1750s, eventually took his earnings, retired, and bought a farm with a house and 100 acres. He set up a garden about a quarter-mile from the house and began to spend all his free time on the property.

Trollop devoted himself to the construction of a little round house placed on the edge of a lake. The cottage became home to an assembly of curios that he had collected over the years. It had a door and window on the front and wood exterior walls described as "a great overcoat of boards," but its most distinctive feature was that it rotated. According to Jessopp's story, "this palace of delights was fixed in some miraculous way on a table and it turned upon a swivel" concealed beneath the building. "Having exercised his genius for many years upon this splendid palace and park of his, he acquired a very wide renown.

People used to come for miles to pay Mr. Trollop a visit."

But visitors who found the cottage in the garden still had to get inside. When Trollop saw someone coming, he would turn its blank backside to the path:

> The would-be visitors, after knocking at the overcoat for a while, would be greeted by the voice of old Bright bidding them to go round to the door, which they never found until he was pleased to give his revolving house a turn, then the door came into sight, and old Bright stood looking out of the window laughing at the gentlefolks.

Trollop made leaving no easier. As the time for the visitor to depart approached, Trollop would rotate the house so that the front faced the very edge of the lake and the let the door be opened. When his guests protested, "the creaking 'of that there swivel' began again," and the visitors could escape onto solid ground.

Two hundred years after Mr. Trollop's death, no known remnants of his rotating house have survived in the Norfolk countryside, so it is impossible to know whether Jessopp's story of the "uncanny devices of the wizard and all the perils of The Folly" was truthful, embellished, or entirely fabricated.[19] Whether real or invented, the story confirms the historic place for a rotating structure in the garden; it also established several themes relating to the revolving house that take clearer shape in the twentieth century: the independent inventor toiling away in solitude on his peculiar vision and the use of the house to amuse and impress visitors.

Rotating Theaters and Auditoria

Around 60 BC Gaius Scribonius Curio, High Priest of the Roman Republic, was said to have developed a theater in which two crescent-shaped wood-framed seating areas were oriented back-to-back and then rotated (with the audience aboard) so that they formed an enclosed amphitheater. Though considerable attention has been paid to how Curio's theater might have functioned, it is unlikely that it was ever constructed. A millennia and a half later, Tommaso Francini, a Renaissance-era engineer specializing in hydraulic garden features, was said to have designed a revolving stage for a grand performance for Louis XIII at the Louvre.

While revolving stages did not find immediate favor in the West, they were used widely and to sophisticated ends in the traditional Japanese theater form, Kabuki. Called *mawari-butai*, revolving stages were introduced by dramatist Namiki Shozo in the 1750s. The earliest versions were simple circular wheeled platforms set on the fixed stage and turned by hand. In time, the turntable was set flush with the stage and the wheels and other machinery were placed beneath. More elaborate versions introduced in the 1820s had two revolving stages, one placed inside the other.[20]

Sometimes the stage was rotated in the dark between scenes to reveal new settings or characters, but it could also be turned in the middle of an act to transition from one scene to the next or to more naturally depict movement of characters, objects, or backgrounds within a scene. Rings of inner and outer rotating stages could depict dynamic events such as the passing of two boats

SECTION OF CURIO'S PIVOTED THEATER.

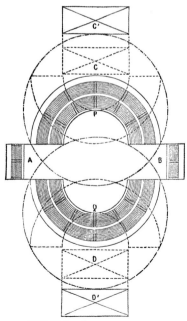

PLAN OF CURIO'S PIVOTED THEATER.

TOP: Nineteenth-century interpretation
of Curio's theater, section LEFT: Curio's theater,
plan RIGHT: Revolving stage, or mawari-butai,
at a Kabuki theater, ca. 1800

in opposite directions. Kabuki historian A. C. Scott describes the effects enabled by the mawari-butai:

> The fundamental feature of the revolving stage is the fact that it allows a whole scene to be changed before the eyes of the audience: time, place and atmosphere can be altered and the sequence of a story carried forward without a break. On the other hand, the audience can be transported back to a point where the story was left off so that it is possible to gain a three-dimensional understanding of the play and its action.[21]

The revolving stage was one of many ingenious scenic devices typically employed in Kabuki theater. Along with stage traps and lifts, sliding doors, rolling wagons, and platforms jutting into the seating area, the mawari-butai drew the audience into the narrative and turned the performance into a shared experience between spectator and actor. With these tools Kabuki dramatists could dynamically reveal transformation and change, depict the supernatural, present exciting entrances and exits, stretch and contract space and time, and extend action beyond the confining walls of the theater. Revolving stages furthered the stylized events characteristic of Kabuki while simultaneously lending naturalism and realism to depictions of movement.

In America early examples of revolving stages in the late 1800s were primarily temporary or portable devices made for specific performances and transported from one theater to the next. Vaudeville acts called "living pictures" or "tableaux vivants" used rotating disks placed on regular stationary stages. The turntables were divided into four, six, or eight sections and rotated during the performance to bring a succession of new scenes before the audience. One well-known company, the Mestayer Musical Comedy Troupe, used a portable rotating stage in one of their productions, which toured all over the eastern and midwestern United States.

Harry Mestayer's group premiered their new farce *We, Us & Co.* in 1884.[22] The "musical absurdity" follows the exploits of a physician named Dr. Pulsiver. Luring his patients to the Mud Springs Spa, Pulsiver vies with several for the affections of a beautiful young woman under his care. The final act is set in and around a revolving house at the spa. One reviewer described it as "an ingenious mechanical contrivance, [that] can be turned in any direction, and the accommodating landlady can provide a north or south room for every guest."[23] In the story the house was set on a decommissioned locomotive turntable and rotated by either a windlass or mule. After the beauty convinces her suitors to don Highland costumes and serenade her with bagpipes, each grabs a ladder to reach her window. "But as they are about to cinch [sic] the prize the house revolves and the fair one eludes them."[24]

Charles Barnard, a journalist, author, and playwright who collaborated with Harry Mestayer, was credited with the idea for this revolving hotel. In his previous job as a scientific editor for popular magazines, Barnard reviewed a variety of inventions that later served as inspiration for his humorous short stories and plays. Barnard's contribution to *We, Us & Co.* helped his career take off and

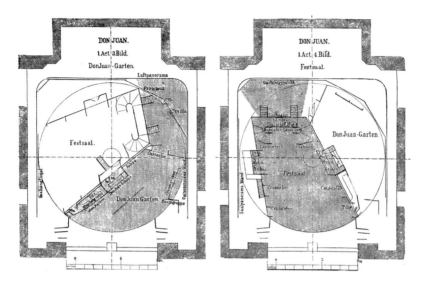

Plan by Karl
Lautenschläger
showing different
rotating stage
configurations for
a performance of
Don Juan

resulted in another production that continued the introduction of new modes of expressing motion and movement on the theater stage. According to an art magazine from the period, "the mechanical ingenuity of the piece attracted the attention of a number of actors in search of novelties, and resulted in an arrangement…by which 'The County Fair' with its tread-mill race-track was produced."[25]

We, Us & Co. is an early presentation of rotating architecture as a misguided advancement of technology at odds with how buildings were defined and used. A spa that turned was considered just another dubious remedy, little different than a quack's cure-all patent medicine. However, the appearance of the Mud Springs Spa would be easier to dismiss as a mere comedic tool had real examples of rotating houses employed at therapeutic resorts and sanatoria not appeared less than twenty years later.

Like Kabuki stages, Mestayer's rotating spa was integrated into the performance and its motion was witnessed as part of the act by the audience. But when permanently installed rotating stages did catch on in Europe and the United States at the end of the nineteenth century, they were primarily functional tools that served behind the curtain. In part they were a response to a perceived crisis many thought the theater was experiencing at the time; to critics audiences seemed bored and detached from performances that were staid and remote. As sets got more elaborate, the duration of the breaks between acts and scenes grew interminable. It was thought that by shortening the intermissions, the dramatic mood would be better preserved.

In 1883 American Charles Needham patented a revolving stage, but it appears the design was never built. The master machinist at New York City's Fifth Avenue Theater proposed a different type of rotating theater considered the first permanent revolving stage in Western theater. Built in 1896, the stage provided quick scenery changes while also reducing the number of stagehands needed behind the curtain. A turntable fifty feet in diameter was set on rollers directly atop the existing stage floor. It could be partitioned into quarters, thirds, or halves or left as an open stage, depending on the production. Lautenschläger was testing the viability of his idea while considering more elaborate versions with multiple lower levels that could accommodate traps and platforms.

Rotating Jails

In December 1880 Indianapolis architect Benjamin F. Haugh arrived at a meeting of the Montgomery County commissioners in Crawfordsville, Indiana, bearing plans for four different jail designs. Administrators had gathered to discuss constructing a new jail that would serve the growing county, and Haugh was co-owner of an iron foundry that developed storefronts and jails.[27] It is not known what other versions the architect proposed that day, but the following spring the commissioners picked what surely must have been the most unusual. On the exterior the building was nondescript—a brick Victorian residence for the sheriff with a square cellblock wing on the rear—but inside the wing there was a completely unique two-story barrel-shaped iron cell block that rotated on a central column. Construction was completed in 1881.

The Montgomery County Jail's cylindrical cell block was divided into sixteen wedge-shaped iron plate cells, eight per level. Each cell originally contained one cot along

Lautenschläger's proposed rotating stage machinery with multiple sublevels

device the following decade. Also unrealized, it called for an annular stage that rotated around the auditorium perimeter but was visible only at the proscenium opening. Using this configuration, several different three-dimensional sets could be built at points on the stage, concealed until needed, and quickly rotated into view.[26]

German stage architect Karl Lautenschläger's basic apparatus at the Munich Court and Residence Theatre is

the wall and a toilet and ventilation grate set into the narrow edge near the center. The central shaft contained a trough for flushing the toilets, ventilation ductwork, and a hollow core that later functioned as a smokestack for the basement furnace. The bars along the curving outer edge had an opening for each cell. The cylinder containing the cells was set into a circular cage of bars with a single opening. For someone to enter or exit a cell, the entire cell-block cylinder had to be rotated so that the opening on the inner cell lined up with the door on the outer cage.

Descriptions of the rotary jail noted that it was to rotate continually throughout the night. In addition to providing an easy means for a single jailor to observe the cells from a fixed vantage point, continual motion prevented the moving inmates from sawing through the bars of the outer cage. Power for turning the drum was to be provided by a water mill or weight-and-spring device. However, it seems that continual rotation was more sales pitch than reality. All of the jails appear to have been turned by means of a hand crank (no easy feat considering the iron cell block weighed many tons).

While the Crawfordsville jail was under construction, Haugh and his architect partner William H. Brown obtained a patent for their design. In the following decade, rotary jails were built from Vermont to West Virginia to the Utah Territory. Designs varied: some had a single level, others had three tiers of cells; in early versions the cylindrical cell block was supported by the central column while in later iterations the cell block was suspended from above. In the late 1880s Haugh and his partners sold their patent to the Pauly Jail

TOP: Exterior of sheriff's residence and rotary jail (right) in Crawfordsville, Indiana
BOTTOM: Basement and central column of the rotary jail in Crawfordsville, 2006 photos

LEFT: Hand crank and entrance to the rotary jail in Crawfordsville, Indiana, 2006 photo **RIGHT**: Rotary jail, Council Bluffs, Iowa, ca. 1970

Company of St. Louis, Missouri. By one count eighteen rotary jails were built across the country by Haugh, Pauly, and others that licensed the design or developed their own variation.[28]

Patentees and manufacturers were certain they were developing a distinct improvement over traditional jail space. The rotary jails were touted as well ventilated and, with toilets in the cells, hygienic. Pauly considered the rotary jail a premier member of their product line. Their catalog stated "there is perhaps no invention of the present age, connected with the construction of jails and other prisons, which has attracted so much attention among those interested in that subject as the Rotary Jail, which for large jails is without doubt the ne plus ultra."[29]

However, many communities experienced buyer's remorse (some within a few years) after constructing their rotary jail.

The drawbacks were numerous. Unimpeded observation, purportedly a main goal of the design, could only be achieved while the cell-block cylinder remained in motion. Ground settlement beneath several jails tilted the cell block out of balance so that it pressed against one side of the circular sleeve and became difficult or impossible to operate. Fire marshals and prison inspectors became increasingly concerned about the hazards of having only one door for all the cells and a contiguous central core that could rapidly spread any fire throughout the structure. Furthermore, broken bones were common among sleeping, inattentive, or incapacitated inmates unfortunate enough to have limbs wedged in the bars when the cylinder was set in motion. In 1904 a prisoner named Charles Fry was killed at the Maryville, Missouri, jail when his head was crushed between the moving bars.[30]

Uncooperative inmates also caused unique problems. A regular prisoner of the Montgomery County Jail named Pegleg had a habit of wedging his wooden limb between the fixed outer bars and the inner bars of the rotating cell block. The sheriff got tired of buying replacement limbs for those shattered when the block was set in motion, so he eventually required Pegleg to surrender his prosthetic leg before being locked up.[31] Demands by grand juries, judges, and health and safety officials to shut down the rotary jails continued into the 1960s. To extend their use, some, like the Montgomery County Jail, were modified to function as normal stationary jails. The inner cell block was spot welded in place, and doors were cut for each cell. Other rotating jails were demolished.

With inmates in the center and the jailor on the periphery, rotary jails were often likened to inverse versions of Jeremy Bentham's design for the Panopticon prison house. An English philosopher and social reformer, Bentham first shared his concept in a series of letters published in 1787. The plan for the round, six-story circular structure had cells arranged around the entire perimeter of the building. A central chamber on each floor allowed jailors to see into each barred cell. However, slots prevented inmates from seeing the jailors and thus knowing if or when they were being observed. Though elements of the Panopticon were incorporated into later prison designs, Bentham was unable to get one built according to his specifications.

Bentham was not the first to introduce the idea of surveillance to prison architecture, but while earlier designs used observation as a means of security, the Panopticon introduced pervasive surveillance as means of enforcing a broader system of behavior and morality. Work was to be required of each inmate within their cells. Supervision would prevent prisoners (with their innately weak minds) from acting on damaging impulses. As one historian has noted, "the benevolence of inspection was in its capacity to prevent transgressions ever taking place. Careless infractions were to be controlled by eliminating all temptation and by making discovery certain."[32] Bentham thought the theory was equally applicable to hospitals, factories, schools, nurseries, and orphanages.[33] This means of social control and behavior modification through surreptitious observation was explored by French postmodernist Michel Foucault, who drew parallels between Bentham's Panopticon and contemporary society's emphasis on controlling behavior through numerous forms of surveillance.[34]

Both the rotary jail and the Panopticon limited contact among inmates and between inmates and jailors. Their designs allowed for reduced staffing, and thus were promoted as being less costly to operate. Bentham intended to use concealed monitoring to mold the morals and character of the prisoners for their supposed benefit; in contrast, the rotary jail featured explicit and regular monitoring that met the needs of jailor first and foremost.

Seeing the problems communities encountered with their revolving jails, it can

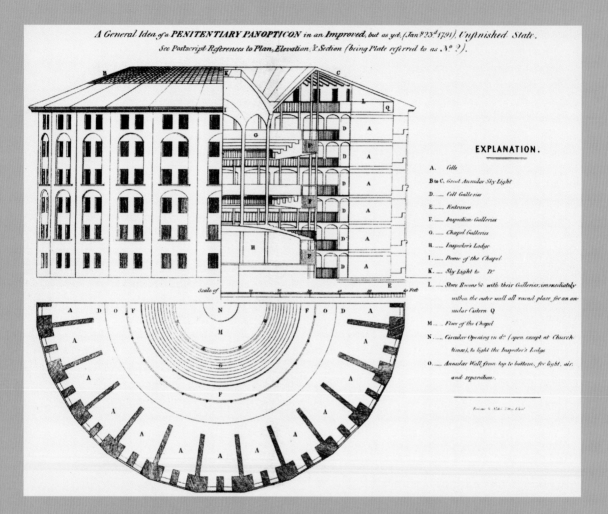

Jeremy Bentham's Panopticon
penitentiary, ca. 1790

be difficult to appreciate the original allure of the concept. Purportedly low operating costs and security were clearly attractive features. Some consider rotary jails a panicked response to the mob violence, robberies, and influx of confidence men that accompanied the rapid settlement of America's Midwest in the late nineteenth century. They also appear to be the product of an era enamored with new mechanical contrivances. County commissions deciding on new jail designs were drawn to the high-tech approach that promised much more than it could deliver. While they offered some conveniences (running water, indoor toilets) that were unprecedented in jail construction, in the end rotary jails came to be viewed as failed architecture and as a failure of the idea that technology would always provide a solution that was in the best interests of humankind. Reflecting this equivocal view of progress, historian Walter Lunden observed in 1959, "maybe the mechanical ingenuity which created the rotary jail is but a part of that same skill which had constructed the man-of-war the *Monitor* with its revolving turret and the rotary action of the Gatling gun adopted by the United States Army after the end of the Civil War."[35]

Rotating Attractions

Vision and observation were instrumental in the creation of other types of facilities and machinery that became popular in the 1800s not for social control but for entertainment. Panoramas, rides, and attractions presented for mass consumption views that were once, in one way or another, restricted. Through rotation, these attractions added a new dimension of excitement and linked views

with the cultural interest in motion and the machine. Invented in Europe in the late 1700s, panoramas began to appear in Western countries throughout the succeeding century. These enormous paintings were masterly displays of perspective, typically presenting a 360-degree cylindrical view of a tourist destination, natural setting, or important historic site or event. They were exhibited in a space organized to encourage the perception that the viewers were immersed within the scene. Lighting and setting were carefully controlled to complement the illusion. Visitors would enter from below, coming up into the center of the cylinder to a skylit promontory within the space that allowed the viewer to see the painting on all sides.

In the United States the panorama was met with less enthusiasm than in Europe. Instead, Americans preferred moving versions, in which a scene was painted on a long strip of canvas, placed on large rollers, and cranked across the view of the audience.[36] In this way the viewer could take a vicarious journey down the Hudson River or across a capital city without leaving his seat and for a low admission cost. Such an attraction opened up the experience of travel and presented new ways of seeing the world to a broad section of the population. In his book about the panorama phenomenon, Stephen Oettermann describes how these attractions democratized perceptions of the landscape visually—making all viewing points equal and without distortion—and politically— as they often depicted sights from formerly privileged perspectives, such as the rooftop of the Louvre.[37] With moving panoramas the sensation of motion, and its association with travel, was re-created with paintings and stage machinery. Real motion and the use of machines to present new vistas were also seen in the variety of attractions developed for fairs, expositions, and resort parks.

While technological innovations were applied first to mills, factories, and railroads, they also found their way to places of play and recreation. In the latter nineteenth and early twentieth centuries the era's penchant for frenetic movement was indulged at the seaside resort and urban amusement park. There, thrill seekers subjected themselves to all sorts of gyrations, twists, and spins, enmeshed in the enormous gears, wheels, and cables of amusement-ride machinery. Switchbacks, roundabouts, merry-go-rounds, sinuous pleasure railways, and roller coasters connected humans to the dynamism of technology. For a nickel or dime these devices provided novel experiences and simulations of the unsafe.

Though similar wood versions called "up-and-downs" date to the eighteenth century, it wasn't until the 1890s that the rides that came to be called Ferris wheels were redesigned on a larger scale using modern engineering. Inventor William Somers introduced his steam-powered Observation Roundabout in 1891, first at Atlantic City and then at Coney Island and Asbury Park. But the concession for a wheel to be constructed for the 1893 World's Columbian Exposition in Chicago went to George Washington Gale Ferris Jr., who developed an enormous structure that was over 250 feet tall and carried 2,400 passengers at a time in thirty-six gondolas. It made one complete revolution per hour.

Ferris wheels transported patrons high above the other attractions and provided unprecedented views of the surrounding landscape. Around 1890 a part-time Methodist preacher named Jesse Lake invented a new attraction for Atlantic City—the revolving observation tower—that promised a similar experience. A native of Pleasantville, New Jersey, Lake had been fascinated with machinery and technology since his youth. He had previously invented a tracked vehicle that anticipated the Caterpillar tractor, a method of allowing passengers to board trains traveling at full speed, and the Haunted Swing, an amusement ride in which passengers sat in a stationary car set within a large box decorated to appear like the interior of a house. The box was tilted and then swung upside down, providing the sensation that the car was spinning within the house.

THIS PAGE
Razzle Dazzle amusement ride, Coney Island, ca. 1896; rotation was provided by hand

OPPOSITE
George Ferris's wheel at the 1893 World's Columbian Exposition in Chicago

Copyrighted by
Geo. Waterman 1893

LEFT: Jesse Lake's Haunted Swing, showing the illusion produced by a ride in the swing
RIGHT: True position of the swing

Lake's steel-framed observation tower stood 125 feet high. A passenger car with benches and a canvas awning ringed the tower and slowly rotated as it ascended and descended during the ten-minute ride. At the tower base, a twenty-six horsepower steam engine provided electrical power for the machinery and thousands of colored lights threaded through the tower and car. A pavilion at the entrance housed various amusements, games, and exhibitions, including films and wax-work shows. Around 1895, Lake built two of the towers near the Boardwalk and purportedly in locations on the Pacific coast.[38] He never patented the invention, so others introduced minor variations and secured the rights to the design.

In 1897 Englishman Thomas Warwick returned from a visit to the United States with a new American wife and the rights to build in Great Britain rotating observation towers that were essentially identical to Lake's design. Warwick erected the first one in Yarmouth, a resort town. After a decade of operation, and with the construction of new attractions along the shore, the tower's novelty waned. World War 1 blackout requirements (imposed for fear of zeppelin attack) prevented the tower from opening after dusk, cutting further into profits. During the war, the mechanism that rotated the car was damaged and effectively abandoned by the tower's owners. Though it continued to operate as an observation tower

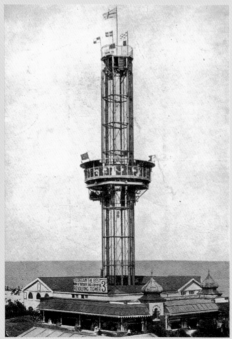

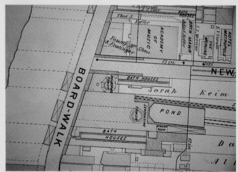

TOP: Jesse Lake's Revolving Tower provided a constantly changing view of Atlantic City's Boardwalk and beach, ca. 1895 **RIGHT**: Map of Atlantic City's Boardwalk showing the Revolving Tower **LEFT**: Revolving tower in Yarmouth, England, based on Lake's design

REVOLVING TOWER,
SOUTHEND ON SEA.

Revolving Tower
at Southend-on-Sea,
England, ca. 1900

during the interwar years, the structure was demolished in 1941 and the metal recycled as part of the national war effort. Between 1895 and 1905 five other revolving towers were built along the English coast. The Yarmouth tower, however, was the only one to survive more than a decade.

Offering the chance to gaze down as the sights slowly turned into and out of view, Jesse Lake's tower was an obvious precursor to the revolving restaurants that would become popular seventy years later. Along with the Ferris wheel, the revolving observation towers became icons for their locations, were featured prominently on postcards, and were undoubtedly used as landmarks for beach goers and boardwalkers looking to meet up with friends or family. The towers turned a previously unavailable view into a marketable commodity. Their winding cable wheels, revolving seating areas, and exposed steel structure were conspicuous examples of the machinery that had been introduced in the nineteenth century and was becoming a pervasive feature of modern life.

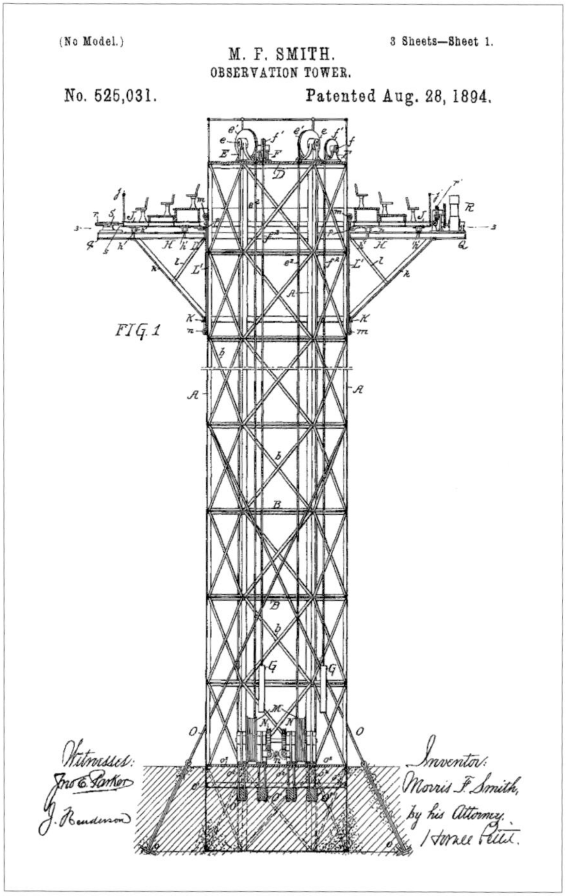

Revolving Houses

In 1883 French caricaturist and novelist Albert Robida published the first in a trilogy of illustrated futuristic novels. *The Twentieth Century* predicted a future of comfort and social equality made possible by nineteenth-century industry and innovation. But in Robida's vision, technological progress is not entirely altruistic. The military is a leading inventor, and the land and water has been contaminated, forcing human life up above the old city's rooftops. Robida's writings were remarkably prophetic. He anticipated

(No Model.)   3 Sheets—Sheet 1.

M. F. SMITH.
OBSERVATION TOWER.

No. 525,031.   Patented Aug. 28, 1894.

FIG. 1

Witnesses:
Jno E. Parker
J. Henderson

Inventor:
Morris F. Smith,
by his Attorney,
Horace Pettit.

the television, national parks, widespread air travel, and aerial and chemical warfare.

In Robida's vision of futuristic life in Paris, houses that combine the appearance of chateaus and train carriages are constructed on circular platforms placed atop existing dwellings. The platform is rotated by a servant immediately below using a hand crank, and the tail or fin extending diagonally from the bottom of the rotating section is similar to those seen on post mills. According

Patent for a revolving tower based on Jesse Lake's design; note the turntable and its wheeled underside that rotates around the upper face of the platform.

to the author, the rooftop rotating house is necessary because most transportation in the twentieth century would be done in dirigible-like flying machines called aerocabs and aeroyachts that would be boarded at roof level, and the growth of the Parisian population and pollution would force new construction ever higher.

An American satirist writing less than a decade after Robida presented the revolving house not as a future necessity but as the inspiration of an eccentric tinkerer. In 1890 the *Boston Globe* printed the presumably fictional story describing a rotating house that was powered by an enormous wound spring. This "whirligigal dwelling," like a giant clockwork, turned slowly throughout the day, keeping preferred rooms filled with sunlight. However, as the designer showed his invention to a visitor, there was a loud crash, and the house started to accelerate. The guest recalled the ensuing events stating, "then I knew the giant mainspring had broken loose, or something of that sort, and was causing the otherwise fairly staid and sensible house to indulge in a wild and delirious waltz. Faster and faster we flew, until finally the sunshine seemed to come in at the window in a steady sheet of blazing light."[39] The inventor is portrayed as a semi-crazed mechanical fetishist whose attempts to realize his vision almost prove fatal.

The same year the *Globe* ridiculed the concept, an engineer from Brooklyn, New York, patented a rotating Tornado Proof Building, a design incorporating a gear he originally developed for swing bridges. Dudley Blanchard's house design was narrow, with one end coming to a point like the bow

of a ship and the rear affixed with a vane. It would sit on a central pivot-point and wheels along the outer edges would ride a circular track on the ground. When the house was buffeted by a storm, winds would push it off blocks and the house would pivot its leading edge into the wind, reducing the chance of being damaged.[40] Newspapers and magazines in the United States and abroad that mentioned Blanchard's design included a gently

OPPOSITE

Rotating house on a rooftop in Paris, as envisioned by Albert Robida in his 1883 book *The Twentieth Century*

THIS PAGE

Dudley Blanchard's 1890 patent for a Tornado Proof Building

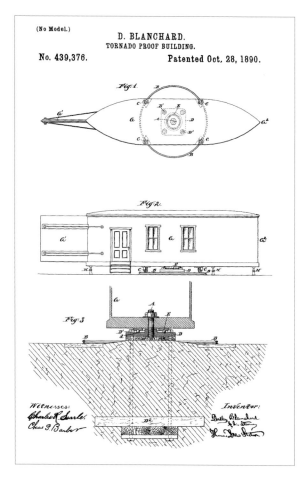

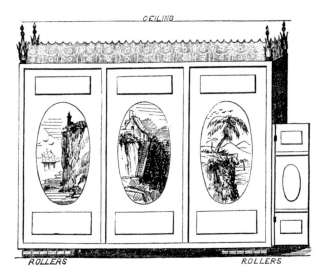

CEILING

ROLLERS   ROLLERS

Design for a movable partition to subdivide rooms, from Catharine Beecher and Harriet Beecher Stowe's 1869 book *The American Woman's Home*

depending on immediate functional requirements and weather conditions.

Partitions set on turntables have also been used historically to mediate between two, often oppositional, places. These modest apparatus served to conceal, to divide, or to regulate contact. Nineteenth-century accounts by American travelers described European orphanages and convents with age-old rotating devices that enabled food or other items to be passed inside by unseen hands. In 1853, renowned traveler John Ross Browne described a Sicilian foundling hospital that had:

> a hole in the wall large enough to admit a good-sized bundle, inside of which is a revolving machine, such as they use in post-offices for the delivery of letters, with four compartments; each large enough to hold a bambino. The unfortunate mother, who is either unable or unwilling to support her offspring, rolls it up in a small package, which she carries to the pigeon-hole at night, thrusts it in, gives the revolving baby-holder a turn, and departs with all possible speed.[41]

mocking appraisal of the type of man who would propose such a house.

In the twentieth century these proposals for rotating houses that turned in their entirety were joined by a second type, the internally rotating residence. Internally rotating homes featured a turntable with two or more partitioned sections, each devoted to a distinct function—usually one incorporated kitchen facilities or another bed, dining table, or couch. The platform could be turned to alternate which section faced the main living space, in effect repurposing that space to meet the occupants' immediate needs. This reorientation of interior rooms has a long history. From the shoji screens of a traditional Japanese house to French doors to the pocket doors and wheeled panels in nineteenth-century American homes, moveable partitions were used to open up, close off, expand, contract, and reprogram interior spaces

Such devices are ancestors to the revolving door, patented first in Germany in the 1880s, which limits air and noise transfer between interior and exterior.

Rotation as a means of controlling contact continued with dumbwaiters and other serving devices, which allowed prepared food to be delivered to dining rooms while servants and slaves were kept out of sight. Thomas Jefferson had a "revolving serving door" constructed just outside of his dining room at Monticello. Appearing like an ordinary panel door on one side, it was set on a pivot and when turned revealed an opposite side with shelves that could accommodate trays, dishes, and glasses. It was similar to a spring-operated design Jefferson installed in the White House during his presidency.[42] A revolving clothes rack set in an alcove at the foot of his bed at Monticello allowed him easy access to numerous coats and waistcoats stored in a restricted space. His rotating desk, a variation of the reading desk designed by Agostino Ramelli, enabled the rapid consultation of several books without rearranging himself or his workspace.

Jefferson's goal of an efficiently run home was taken up in the nineteenth century by many social reformers, architects, and amateur inventors. Plans and tools were developed to rationalize and reduce the amount of labor expended on household work as women became more involved in the creation of their own workplaces and as domestic servants became increasingly rare. This movement to reshape kitchens and other female domestic spaces to make them more efficient and reduce the amount of movement required by the housewife was reflected in an invention by a millinery shop proprietor named Elizabeth Howell. In 1891 Howell

was the first to patent what she named a "self waiting table" and what later came to be called the "lazy Susan."[43] Exhibited at the 1893 Columbian Exposition in Chicago, this simple assembly of a revolving disk set into the middle of a table or placed atop a table could be laden with food and slowly turned to deliver different dishes to individual diners.

Through the end of the nineteenth century rotating houses remained the realm of the dreamer. They were envisioned as an inevitable form for future city life, made necessary by forthcoming revolutions in mobility and transportation and a continual reduction in available urban space. They were the products of brilliant but probably off-balance minds. The few discussions of revolving houses were suffused with cautionary reminders that such a concept was a striking departure from past building design. As Albert Robida wrote in his character's voice, "What was natural and logical to our good and down-to-earth ancestors became impractical to us."[44] These characterizations and concerns appeared again in the following century as successive generations continued to grapple with the place of technology in everyday life and the use and meaning of rotating structures.

CHAPTER TWO

ROTATING ARCHITECTURE 1900–1945

········ ── ─────···

The rapid pace of technological innovation seen in the nineteenth century increasingly came to define life in the succeeding century. Electricity brought push-button automation into the home and with it the promise of gadget-enabled ease and convenience.[1] Machinery as well as factory and household labor were honed for efficiency. Earlier innovations like power-generating dynamos and steam locomotives were joined by the automobile and airplane. The revolution in mechanical motion emphasized mobility and constant change, themes that carried over into literature, the arts, industrial design, and architecture. Contemporary designers developed forms that expressed movement and speed. Streamlined office buildings and theaters assumed the aerodynamic look of airplanes, while early modernist homes borrowed metal rails and deck-like balconies from steamships. In the 1920s the Swiss architect Le Corbusier published his famous assertion that "a house is a machine for living in" and claimed "in the name of the steamship, the airplane, and the automobile, the right to health, logic, daring, harmony, perfection."[2]

To their designers, rotating buildings were a practical application of the latest technology, from motors to rolling-element bearings. Early twentieth-century rotating designs adapted and expanded space, whether in the driveway, the urban apartment, or the theater. They enabled homeowners and therapists to regulate contact with the world outside. They provided dramatic views to fairgoers and novelty to bar goers. Architectural theorists and avant-garde artists used them more symbolically, as dynamic harbingers of the future. But as early as 1908 some critics thought the largely untried concept was already dated and insufficiently modern to match such a mobile era. Charles DeKay, in *American Architect & Building News*, wrote:

> Ours is the age of frantic movement, of steamships and railways, automobiles and flying machines. The world is turning nomadic again. We may soon find that the architect who wishes to keep up with the times will have to devise a moveable house, not a mere revolving house, but one which can take the road and supply the modern craving for a purely physical, mindless getting-along-through space![3]

Rotating devices explicitly connected architecture to new technologies of movement. Turntables were placed in garages,

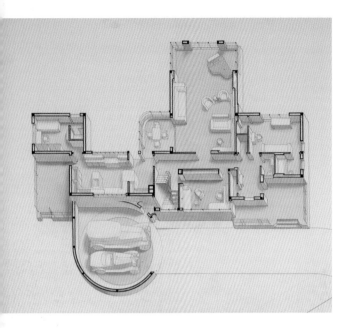

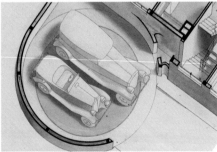

ABOVE AND RIGHT:
Norman Bel Geddes
House Number 3
with its turntable
garage, designed for
*Ladies' Home
Journal*, 1930

aerodynamic, mechanical aesthetic. Turntable garages synthesized the automobile and the home, blurring the line between structure and machine.[5] Another influential industrial designer, Raymond Loewy, adapted a turntable to quickly and efficiently move automobiles around his Rotary Servicenter. The 1934 gas station was completely enclosed in a streamlined building clad in red, white, and blue porcelain enamel panels. Over a two-minute revolution, a team of attendants filled cars with gas, oil, water, and air. Demonstrating the design's intended use in built-up urban areas, Esso Corporation constructed two of the Servicenters in New York City.[6]

A similar concept was employed by the Walker-Gordon Company in 1930 with their development of the Rotolactor milking parlor, a design motivated by their desire to increase efficiency while keeping milk sterile from the udder to the bottle. The structure provided space for simultaneously milking ten to twenty cows. Upon entering a stanchion on the slowly moving turntable, the cow was cleaned and attached to the milking machine. As it rotated the machine extracted the milk and sent it through the pasteurization and bottling process. After a cow completed its rotation, milked and cleaned again, it was returned to its stall in the (stationary) barn. A smaller version of the Rotolactor was exhibited at the New York World's Fair in 1939, housed inside a streamlined building titled "The Dairy World of Tomorrow." After the fair, this same facility was moved to Walker-Gordon's Needham, Massachusetts, farm, where it remained in use until 1960.

driveways, and service courts, enabling automobiles to enter and exit in forward gear.[4] The 1930 drawings for House Number 3 that industrial designer Norman Bel Geddes prepared for the *Ladies' Home Journal* featured a two-car turntable in a circular garage projecting from the front of the building. The extensive glazing, smooth stucco, and rounded corners provided an emphatic articulation of the design's overall

LEFT: Esso Rotary Servicenter by Raymond Loewy, New York City, ca. 1934
BOTTOM: Rotary Servicenter interior, New York City; note the crowd of curious onlookers on the street outside.

WALKER-GORDON "ROTOLACTOR"

Walker-Gordon's Rotolactor, 1952 postcard
Lake County (IL) Discovery Museum/Curt Teich
Postcard Archives

The same year Norman Bel Geddes developed his House Number 3 he also worked on a series of drawings for a rotary airport proposed for construction in New York Harbor. It looked like an enormous aircraft carrier, with a flat deck accommodating two runways along the edges and a terminal hall sitting atop a central concrete pinion. The deck, equivalent in area to seven city blocks, would float on a series of ballasted buoyancy tanks. It was to be turned on the pinion by marine propellers beneath the surface so that the runways could be aligned with prevailing winds for optimal take-off and landing conditions.[7]

Like Bel Geddes and Raymond Loewy, the inventors of some rotating structures were professional industrial designers, architects, and engineers. Occasionally they worked with experts from other professions—physicians, stage directors. In some cases they were articulating the whims of an eccentric client; in others, they were developing a highly personal vision for their own use. A significant number of rotating structures, however, were developed by inventors with no previous design experience.

The years between 1890 and 1920 were the golden age of the independent inventor. Self-employed innovators sought patentable solutions and new marketable products in a variety of areas. Following patent developments in technical journals they identified active areas of innovation and, sensing opportunity, threw their designs into the fray.[8] Toiling in basement workshops, often moonlighting, inventors of rotating structures were alternately considered genius visionaries or "of the genus crank."[9] Suggesting a larger

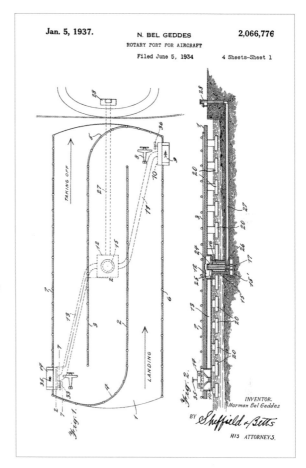

public ambivalence about proposed changes to the traditional concept of home, revolving house designers were lampooned with a special enthusiasm in newspaper and magazine articles.

Drawings from Norman Bel Geddes' rotary airport patent application, 1934

Rotating Theaters

At the beginning of the twentieth century modern revolving stages were in use at several theaters in Europe and the United States. Karl Lautenschläger had built four permanent

TOP: Turntable stage designed to rotate at the same rate as runners depicting a race at the London Coliseum, 1904 MIDDLE: Elaborate control panel for the London Coliseum's revolving stage, ca. 1920 BOTTOM: View of the motor, track, and steel structure beneath the rotating stage at the London Coliseum, ca. 1920

turntable stages in various continental cities. According to one observer, it was "an appliance over which Europe is now going crazy."[10] Other stage designers, most notably Max Reinhardt, continued efforts to reenergize Western theater, in part by employing revolving stages.

Reinhardt's productions were often lavish and grand spectacles that integrated lighting, costume design, sets, stage form, and acting styles into a seamless experience. When he became general manager of the Deutsches Theater in Berlin, Reinhardt built a revolving stage used both for quick changes of elaborate sets and to enable new dramatic effects. Previously in Western theater the revolving stage was usually operated behind a drop curtain. Reinhardt was known to use his revolving stage in a more dynamic manner. During his 1905 production of *A Midsummer Night's Dream* the designer depicted the two settings of court and forest intermingled on a stage that revolved as part of the performance and in full view of the audience.[11] The revolving stage at the London Coliseum was likewise employed for special effects. Illustrations from the period show a running-race scene with the turntable in motion matching the runners' pace so that they remained framed within the proscenium.

The first permanent revolving stage built in the United States was probably at Ye Liberty Playhouse in Oakland, California, in 1903. It was designed by the manager Harry Bishop, who had reportedly seen revolving Kabuki stages during a trip to Japan. The turntable rotated on casters and was 75 feet in diameter, large enough to accommodate a fire engine or fully loaded haywagon. Stagehands rotated the turntable, pushing off from stationary posts at the edge of the stage. According to the opening night playbill, the stage allowed quick set changes between acts and also made "it possible to build up solid scenes on a scale of magnificence heretofore impossible."[12]

In the decades that followed, architects, stage designers, and critics including Pierre Albert-Birot, Oskar Strnad, and Walter Gropius developed plans for reconfigurable and rotating theaters that exploded the established definition of performance spaces. Some, like Strnad's design, had annular stages that encircled and rotated around the audience. Zygmund Tonecki and Szymon Syrkus's 1929 Theatre of the Future had ring stages and circular platform stages that could rotate independently and be raised or lowered during performances. Unfortunately, none of these "total theatre" projects were built.[13]

Rotating Treatment Buildings

In 1903 well-known French architect, M. Eugéne Pettit in consultation with physician Lucien Pellegrin exhibited a rotating "heliotropic house" at the Exposition de l'Habitation in Paris. The model was based on a full-size building called the Villa Tournesol Pettit had constructed in the south of France. Premised on the physician's conviction that the sun was the cure for most diseases, it was often referred to as a "Family Sanatorium." A cross-shaped plan with large window openings on most walls helped get light into the interior. To administer this daylight to different rooms at different times, the house was set on a turntable with a ground-level ball-bearing raceway. It could be rotated to follow the

Pettit and Pellegrin's heliotropic house, 1903

sun by "moving a lever once an hour in order to cause the house to turn a few inches."[14] In a proposed larger version the owners would have the option to install a gasoline engine that could rotate the house once per day.

When the design was publicized in the United States, the New York City health commissioner questioned its feasibility, "but if rotating houses are possible there can be no discussion of their desirability. The sun kills disease germs. Its rays constitute the best disinfectant known." He added that, "above all, sunshine is the one agency most conducive to cheerfulness. It is the cheapest kind of medicine. Rotating houses, constructed to point toward the sun from its rising to its setting, would be rather expensive, but to those who could afford the luxury they would well repay the cost."[15]

The sun has long played a prominent role in health and medicine. In the late 1800s sunbathing was found to be an effective treatment for vitamin D deficiency and rickets. Heliotherapy—treating illnesses by exposing a patient to regulated solar radiation—became a well-established remedy around the turn of the twentieth century for nervous disorders and respiratory diseases, anemia, Hodgkin's disease, septic wounds, syphilis, and tuberculosis of the skin, bones, and joints. Europe was the center of heliotherapeutic research and experimentation as experts established clinics in the Swiss Alps, Germany, and France.

A standard prescription for pulmonary tuberculosis and pneumonia included a regular supply of fresh air. Doctors established for each patient an amount of time they were to be exposed to the air and sun. To facilitate exposure, architects, physicians, and scientists designed sanatoria with terraces and rooms featuring large, operable windows. Though Pellegrin and Pettit's exhibition house seemed drastic at the time, compared to another project by a French physician working in the decades that followed, their design seemed only a half measure.

Jean Saidman was born in Romania but emigrated to France as a teenager. He studied medicine and became an early expert in the field of actinology, a branch of science that explored the chemical effects of light. In the 1920s, through his popular practice, he became a physician "a la mode" among Parisians. In 1929, assisted by architect Andre Farde, Saidman designed and patented a new type of solarium to improve upon existing ultraviolet light treatments. The first version was built in the French spa community Aix-les-Bains the following year, and it looked unlike any building ever constructed.[16]

The design's base (or "pillar") featured ground-floor examination and waiting rooms and a steeply pitched conical roof covered with diamond-shaped tiles. Inside the reinforced concrete base, an elevator and spiral staircase connected the ground floor to a rotating platform above. An electric motor in the basement turned the eighty-ton steel platform, which featured a monitoring and control room in the center and four glass-fronted treatment cabins extending to each side. In his patent Saidman stated that he situated the cabin platform high in the air so that it would be clear of trees and better ventilated.

Each cabin had an adjustable bed and a small changing room at the back. The bed was connected to a motorized assembly of nickel oxide or cobalt glass screens (that blocked specific wavelengths), as well as lenses and lamps that could be moved into various positions above the patient. Depending upon the illness and its prescribed treatment, the lens panel and bed could be configured to direct the sun's rays to specific parts of the body while keeping the patient perpendicular to the sun. Rotation meant, of course, that all the cabins could remain in sunlight throughout the day. Saidman's team used the solarium to treat patients with various forms of rheumatism, dermatosis, tuberculosis, rickets, and cancer.[16]

Jean Saidman's revolving solarium,
Aix-les-Bains, France, ca. 1935; note glass
screening panel in leftmost cabin

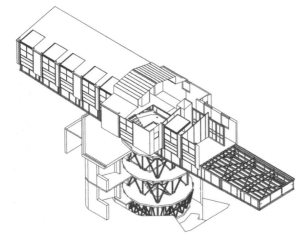

In 1934 Saidman established the Institut Héliothérapique in Vallauris, France. In addition to a large hospital complex designed by architect Pierre Souzy, the Institut featured a solarium modeled after the first version built in Aix-les-Bains. That same year Saidman supervised construction of a third rotating solarium, in Jamnagar, state of Gujarat, India. It was part of the Ranjit Institute of Poly-Radio Therapy, named after its founder, the Maharajah Jam Ranjitsinhji. The Vallauris and Jamnagar solaria featured a two-story octagonal base and an enclosed rooftop meteorological observatory. Although Saidman's patent called for only the top platform to rotate, both of the latter versions were more complicated designs with their upper rotating platform connected to a rotating stairway core that ran through the center of the base and sat on rollers in the basement, where it was connected to an electric motor.

The buildings provided an interesting blend of high-tech and natural treatments. While the chief medicine was solar radiation, the facilities also included state-of-the-art equipment that used X-rays, radium, and infrared lights. This duality of high and low technology was also apparent in Saidman's original design, which remained traditionally residential in appearance at the base while a giant propeller-like pedestal of steel and glass swung above.

Saidman's solarium was a dramatic response to the perceived needs of his patients. But more modest treatment structures were also in use from the beginning of the century. Home owners constructed sleeping porches and rooftop shelters on existing buildings. "Tent houses" and basic bungalows helped to separate patients who had dangerous coughs from the main wards. With removable or sliding sash windows, French doors, canvas curtains, or screens, these buildings balanced the need for fresh air and sunlight with a basic protection from biting winds, rain, and snow. Since these tent houses and cottages were set above ground on posts for better ventilation, it was a simple step to incorporate a turntable and lend them the added benefit of rotation. Around the turn of the century, small encampments of rotating shelters were established on the grounds of hospitals and sanatoria in Britain and continental Europe.

Kelling Sanatorium for Working Men in Norwich, England, had at least a dozen rotating, wood-framed shelters, each equipped with one or two beds, a locker, and a commode. The front sides of the shelters were almost entirely open to the elements, but because they could be turned on a circular iron track away from the wind and into the sun, patients preferred them to the more conventional wards with open sides, which were considered too cold and drafty.[18] Other UK hospitals that used rotating treatment shelters included the City Hospital for Infectious Diseases and the Astley Ainslie Hospital, both in Edinburgh, Scotland. Dr. Karl Turban and Dr. Hans Philippi, two well-known physicians based in Davos, Switzerland, also designed and arranged for the construction of rotating huts for use at their exclusive sanatoria.

Individuals also used treatment shelters at private residences (usually in the garden) to isolate infected loved ones. In the 1926 novel *Confession* by English author Cosmo

OPPOSITE
TOP: Rotating solarium at Jamnagar, India
MIDDLE: Cut-away drawing of the Jamnagar solarium showing the steel structure and rotating central drum **BOTTOM**: Motor and chain drive in the basement of the Jamnagar solarium

THIS PAGE
TOP: Rotating tuberculosis hut adjacent to the fixed wards at City Hospital for Infectious Diseases, Edinburgh, Scotland, 1909 **BOTTOM**: Close-up of rotating tuberculosis hut at City Hospital for Infectious Diseases, Edinburgh, Scotland, 1909

Fresh Air for Patients

B. & P. Shelters enable the most delicate to take the utmost advantage of fresh air and sunshine, whilst strong and cold winds are excluded.

These shelters are designed on an improved principle and can easily be revolved according to the direction of the wind. Size 8 ft. × 6 ft. Sent in sections for easy fixing.

Write for full details and Catalogue A.75

Boulton & Paul Ltd

Telegrams: BOULTON NORWICH **NORWICH** Telephone NORWICH 851 (5 lines)

LONDON OFFICE: 135-137, QUEEN VICTORIA ST. E.C

Telegrams: Boutique. Cent London Telephone 4642 Cent

TOP: Early twentieth-century rotating shelter located in the garden of Jon Lawrence, Kent, England, ca. 2003 LEFT: Advertisement for Boulton & Paul revolving shelter from *British Journal of Tuberculosis*, ca. 1912 RIGHT: Prefabricated Turn-table house produced by E. F. Hodgson & Co., ca. 1910

Hamilton, a character expresses concern for one such patient: "And as for that poor young Cambridge man who lives in a tent on Smith's meadow and is dying of tuberculosis and writes Greek verse between his fits of coughing—it's been wringing my heart to hear him—I've sent to London for one of those large revolving air rooms and asked Mr. Pickering's permission to have it set up on the edge of the woods. He's a charming, whimsical boy, so gentle and hopeful."[19]

The quote reveals the portable nature of these buildings and the fact that they could be ordered and shipped across the country. While some, like those at Kelling Sanatorium, were custom designed, English manufacturers, including Boulton & Paul and G. F. Strawson, offered similarly styled prefabricated rotating shelters for sale to institutions and individuals.[20] Referencing fashionable spas in the Swiss Alps, the houses were often vaguely chalet in style with a small porch on the front and scalloped eaves. Kits were made up of the necessary window sash, metal hardware, and either precut lumber or sectional panels; they were designed to be shipped by rail or truck and assembled by amateur builders.

In the United States at least one firm offered a rotating cottage that was marketed for the treatment of tuberculosis. Based in Dover, Massachusetts, E. F. Hodgson & Company manufactured a variety of prefabricated structures including full-sized residences, garages, playhouses, pony stables, covered sand boxes, and birdhouses. Their Turn-table house consisted of light wood sections that were bolted together for easy assembly. Approximately 7 feet square with

an open front and window on the rear elevation, it provided just enough room for a bed and nightstand or chair. A retractable canvas covering enabled the front opening to be partially or completely closed. The house sat on top of five rollers and was rotated by turning a crank connected to a chain drive.[21]

Catalog illustrations of Hodgson's other structures reveal that the Turn-table house was a modified version of their earlier garden house design. Because their buildings were prefabricated from individual panels, the manufacturer had only to substitute an open panel for the garden house's front entrance and set the structure on a turntable to create a new product that appealed to a new market. Hodgson started promoting the Turn-table house in books and journals covering tuberculosis treatments while the garden house continued to appear in advertisements in popular magazines.

Rotating Summer Houses

As the Hodgson design suggests, rotating treatment cottages were related to, and in many cases adapted from, the age-old summer houses and gloriettes that commonly embellished European ornamental gardens. Alternately known as teahouses or garden houses, these structures provided a sheltered refuge away from the main house where owners and guests could enjoy refreshments and conversation or pause to enjoy a particular view while strolling through scenic surroundings. In the twentieth century they also served as centers for outdoor sports, exercise, and sunbathing. As in the past, garden houses (both stationary and rotating) appealed to the eccentric, the artist, and the

George Bernard Shaw's rotating writing shed

well heeled who sought escape from society or distraction.

Such structures continued to enjoy popularity in Europe and the United States throughout the first half of the twentieth century. In 1911 Mary Leiter, the wealthy widow of department store magnate Levi Leiter, designed a backyard folly for her lavish summer estate in Beverly, Massachusetts.[22] The summer house was located on a small hill on the edge of Massachusetts Bay, about fifty feet from the main house. Square in plan and framed with rustic wood, it had glass walls on three sides and an entrance on the fourth.[23] The floor was covered with imported rugs and the furnishings included "comfortable lounging chairs and dainty little tables."[24] Above, rough-hewn beams formed a pitched roof that was covered with bark shingles.

Pushing a button (presumably connected to an electric motor) set the steel turntable in motion, turning the house so that its occupants could escape cool ocean winds in favor of sheltered sunlight. It was said to be extremely quiet, according to one account, revolving "as noiselessly and gently as it would if commanded by a company of fairies."[25] The house was an amusing, unique plaything that Mary Leiter used to entertain and impress visitors, a place for her to escape the formality of her summer palace. One newspaper noted "it would be difficult for one to find anything among the thousands of luxuries of wealth which would quite eclipse this new and novel miniature toy which has been built at enormous expense for the use of Mrs. Leiter and her guests during their stay in Beverly."[26]

Rotating summer houses seem to have been particularly favored by writers and scholars who desired uninterrupted escape and the opportunity to fine-tune their immediate environment to aid creativity. English physician and social reformer Havelock Ellis and Arthur Rex Knight, a leading professor of psychology, both wrote important works in their revolving summer houses. Irish dramatist George Bernard Shaw appropriated his wife's rotating cottage located in the back garden of their property, Shaw's Corner, in Hertfordshire, England. The prefabricated structure featured a simple shed roof rising from the rear to a front elevation with a pair of windows flanking the door. Shaw converted it for his use by adding electric light, a heater, and a telephone. According to the Shaws' assistant gardener, Fred Drury, the writer found refuge in the solitary and spartan environment located some distance from the main house. Tucked away there writing some of his best-known plays, including *Man and Superman* and *Pygmalion*, he ignored alarm clocks and entreaties from his staff reminding him to return for lunch.[27]

Rotating Buildings and the Avant-Garde

While inventors and tinkerers often saw their rotating designs as an engineered, rational means to regulate sunlight, maximize space, or vary the view, others developed rotating designs that articulated new artistic, political, and philosophical ideas. This trend was especially prevalent in Europe during the first half of the twentieth century—a time when revolutionary styles of painting, graphic design, literature, and architecture were sweeping over the continent. Rotating

Casa Giratoria by Paul Klee, 1921, presents a multifaceted view of a revolving house similar to what avant-garde architects were proposing in the interwar years.

structures reflected dynamic mobility and hope for the future. By overturning traditional assumptions about buildings—that above all they were to be stable and static—revolving designs signaled a dramatic break with the past. They announced an allegiance between architecture and machinery and made explicit the modern faith in progress through technology and movement.

Expressionist architecture originated in Germany and other Central European countries during the first decades of the twentieth century. Not defined by any rigid approach or formal consistency, expressionism encompassed a broad range of forms that shared a common tendency toward plasticity and away from traditional orthogonal design. Bruno Taut, Erich Mendelsohn, and other expressionist architects experimented with "light-kinetic principles" to demonstrate the triumph of time and mobility over space. Some designs featured biomorphic motifs, while others drew inspiration from geologic forms. The end results were often eclectic, highly individual exercises that emphasized emotion, sensation, experience, motion,

and the articulation of symbolic meaning. Mendelsohn's 1920–21 Einstein Tower in Potsdam, Germany, is certainly the best-known expressionist work. A laboratory and observatory for exploring Einstein's theory of relativity, its curving white exterior looked like it has been worn down and rubbed smooth by rushing wind or water.

Expressionism came to the fore in Germany at a tumultuous time—during and after World War 1, when old political orders were swept away. War and the economic crises that followed meant few actual commissions and little construction. As a result, expressionist architecture was articulated most often in sketches and theoretical tracts. Without the opportunity to build, expressionist designs were free from functional requirements, financial restrictions, and limitations of site and material.

Various expressionist designs, both drawn and described, were intended to rotate, though none of these were built. In 1920, Max Taut designed the Rotating House that his brother Bruno Taut published in the short-lived magazine, *Frühlicht* (Dawn).[28] It was to have been constructed six years earlier for a Mr. Mendthal on the sand dunes overlooking the Baltic Sea near Königsberg. The sketch showed zig-zagging glass walls wrapping around a generally cylindrical plan. A series of dormer-like roofs joined these wall sections to a central steeply pitched pyramidal core. Railed balconies circled both the glass walls on the main level and the center core above. Though the site may have played a part, the primary motive for having the design rotate was philosophical. To accentuate the building's whirling dynamism, Taut's drawing had text that described the house spiraling out from its center.

The faceted, glazed walls and spiked roofs of the Rotating House exhibited a close resemblance to the crystalline forms that were a central design motif of much expressionist architecture. Later in 1920, expressionist Carl Krayl developed designs for suspended and swinging architecture, buildings such as the Crystalline Star House that hung from the side of a cliff. With their shimmering faceted panes and folded facades, Krayl's and Taut's crystal designs suggested movement even when stationary.[29]

Concurrent with expressionism, constructivist architecture was a movement unique to the new Soviet Union. Influenced by constructivist art, it gained cultural authority and official sanction in the years following the 1917 Russian Revolution as the new government abandoned traditional forms associated with the imperial past and sponsored works that represented its social and political outlook. As with the expressionists in Germany, constructivist designers worked in a dynamic, heady atmosphere that, because few resources were available for actually building, often turned to utopian architectural fantasy. Their works featured an industrial vocabulary of exposed structural frames, cross bracing, and guy wires. Abstract forms were shaped in concrete, steel, and glass. Revealing a connection to contemporary trends in the plastic arts, constructivist architecture sometimes incorporated kinetic elements that brought to life the sense of motion implicit in many designs.

The best-known example of constructivist architecture is Vladimir Tatlin's Monument

Max Taut's Rotating House from *Frühlicht*, 1920

to the Third International, designed in 1919. It was intended to be the headquarters for the new communist government, as well as an enormous physical symbol of industrial progress, dynamism, and transparency, ideas with which the new regime hoped to be associated. The project never progressed further than sketches and a model exhibited at parades and expositions.

Like the offspring of a union between the Eiffel Tower and a rollercoaster, the monument was to consist of an open iron framework spiraling upward from a wide base to a tight peak. This frame supported and contained three separate glass-walled volumes that were to accommodate various legislative and administrative functions. Each had a different geometric shape and was intended to rotate at a different rate. The lower cubic form would have revolved on its axis once per year, the middle pyramid once per month, and the cylindrical form near the top once each day. In all, the built structure was to measure over 1,300 feet high.[30]

Model of the
Monument to the
Third International,
Vladimir Tatlin,
ca. 1920

The Monument to the Third International was more sculpture than architecture. No serious consideration was apparently given to the practical challenges of erecting such a tower at a time of continued social and economic upheaval. Despite this, the design proved a potent assertion of the new regime's optimistic vitality. Even without the rotating features, the structure would have exuded movement and energy. As with Taut's house, it seemed to be in motion even at rest. The stretched coil of steel lattice-work and rotating internal components drew overt connections to industry and technology, prized by the Bolsheviks as the routes to modernization. Tatlin's monument was a temple to the machine and, through it, the aspirations of a dynamic Soviet Union.

The designs of Taut, Tatlin, and others were utopian dreams steeped in avant-garde artistic currents. Rotation was symbolic, and the practical challenges of turning structures seemed of little interest to the architects. But the first half of the twentieth century also saw numerous designers in Europe and the United States earnestly developing full-size homes meant for year-round occupation that rotated for pragmatic reasons and in ways that were mechanically viable.

The New Rotating House

To many European and American designers working during this period, the time had come for a wholly new type of residential architecture. The machinery and materials to make rotating houses and apartments were readily available; medicine and science seemed to provide ample evidence for the advantages of turning structures; faith in invention and

technology as an engine of progress was widespread. Yet despite the exhortations of experts and the climate of innovation present during the first half of the twentieth century, most rotating home plans never made it beyond the drawing board or the patent office.

Proposals for rotating houses were often met with a mix of curiosity and derision. Newspapers and magazines often featured small one- or two-paragraph write-ups of rotating house designs as "believe it or not" filler pieces. The concept was clearly intriguing. However, the writers' asides and concluding comments, intending to be humorous, often suggest a distinct unease with the idea of a home meant to turn. One article referring to a 1924 German rotating house design stated "there is no knowing as yet, how popular this truly revolutionary conception in architecture may become. Neither is there any news of the fate of the man who forgets to step off the platform before pressing the button—perhaps because it too horrible to contemplate."[31]

The likely root of these mixed feelings is the way rotating houses subverted the traditional concept of the home as a bastion of stability and security. Buster Keaton's 1920 film *One Week* confirmed with slapstick flair prevailing notions of how a house should look and perform. Walls are expected to be straight, the kitchen sink should be on the inside, and above all, the house should remain fixed on its foundations. Keaton's film tells the story of newlyweds who receive a kit house, unassembled in a series of crates. When a jilted and vengeful suitor secretly rearranges the crates, the finished project

TOP: Buster Keaton struggles to stop his house from rotating, still image from 1920 film *One Week*.

BOTTOM: Henry Ford and friends (including Thomas Edison and President Harding) dine efficiently with help from a lazy Susan while camping, 1921.

house designs developed during this period fit within one of two general categories: those with components that turned inside the structure and those where the structure itself turned. Internally rotating houses were a product of the turn-of-the-century efficiency movement and the increasingly crowded conditions in America's cities. Efforts to maximize industrial productivity—to extract the most work in the shortest amount of time using the least amount of energy and material—were initiated by Frederick Winslow Taylor and Henry Ford. Scientific management principles were also applied to domestic spaces and the activities of those who worked there. The American home became a laboratory for rationalization and technological innovation aimed at rooting out waste and systemizing household labor. The "housewife" became a "home engineer." Publications like Christine Frederick's 1915 book *Household Engineering* encouraged the adoption of space-saving, time-saving, and labor-saving processes, devices, and interior layouts—especially in kitchens.[33] At the same time, cities were experiencing unparalleled population growth that was shrinking the size of typical urban apartment units and reducing the average number of rooms in each apartment. Space was at a premium.

Internally Rotating Houses

During the height of the efficiency trend some intrepid designers worked to make residential interiors more functional and adaptable. Wringing the maximum utility from limited square footage, they addressed a perceived drawback to conventional dwellings with rooms dedicated to specific

bears little resemblance to that shown in the instructions. An enormous storm interrupts repair efforts, setting the house spinning in place and throwing the inhabitants along the interior walls and through the windows. Upon making his escape, a survivor remarks, "I had a lovely afternoon on your merry-go-round. It'll be better when you put in your hobby-horses."[32]

Whether actually constructed, feasible but unbuilt, or fanciful concept, the rotating

functions—some rooms were only used for brief periods while the rest of the day this space was unoccupied and essentially wasted. In smaller residences, the dining room table or bed was in the way whenever it wasn't being used.

Foldaway furniture, which originated in Scandinavia in the nineteenth century, came into much more widespread use in the early twentieth century. Folding "door bed" designs appeared that promised rooms could function as parlors by day and bedrooms at night. Frustrated by his small San Francisco apartment, which afforded little space for entertaining, William L. Murphy developed a new fold-up bed design. In 1911 he started to patent and manufacture a line of "disappearing beds" and "wall beds." The company was so successful that his name became the generic trademark by which all foldaway beds are now known.[34] At the same time, other manufacturers offered foldaway dining and breakfast sets, fold-up ironing boards, and concealable footrests for shoe cleaning, all of which easily and quickly customized a single, limited space for a variety of activities. Internally rotating designs took these inventions several steps further, remaking the entire interior of a house and doing away with that most wasteful and inflexible space—the hallway. Inhabitants no longer walked from room to room, but brought the room to them. Unlike the Murphy bed and the fold-up breakfast nook, however, there are no known built examples of any of the many internally rotating residences designed during this period.

A basic design like that described in Los Angeleno Earl Tate's 1914 patent featured a turntable divided into two halves, one with a bed, the other with a table, buffet, and sideboard.[35] When installed as a divider between two rooms, one space would be "used alternately as a reception room, sleeping room, or dining room" while the other was to function "as a kitchen, butler's pantry, and repository for the conveniences when they are not desired in the alternative position."[36]

Four years later Pasquale Cimini of Brooklyn patented a more ambitious design with a four-section turntable that incorporated a dresser, bed, closet, and kitchenette.[37] The latter section was equipped with a washtub and stove, taking on the challenge of adapting fittings and fixtures. To do so the inventor used a system similar to that found in the rotary jails. A central standpipe with revolving connector sections riding on ball-bearing mounts linked the faucets and drains on the turntable to stationary pipes in the building. No mention is made in the patent about how gas was to be supplied to the stove. Like the Tate design, Cimini planned to support his turntable on a grooved ball-bearing track set into the floor structure.

In both of these designs, complicated assemblies of springs, latches, gears, cables, weights, casters, and hinges enabled the turntable's furnishings to extend into the room for use and then retract so the device could be rotated. When at rest, the interior could have an entirely conventional appearance that need not reveal its peculiar capabilities. In fact, the concealed rooms and apparatus of internally rotating designs may have held considerable allure to the inventor. The hidden partitions resembled that popular contrivance of mystery novels—a revolving bookcase that opens

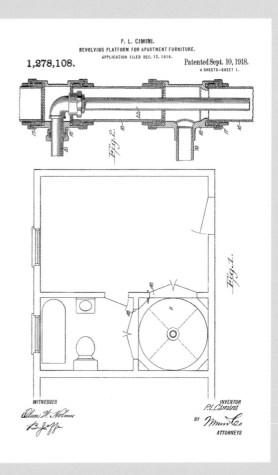

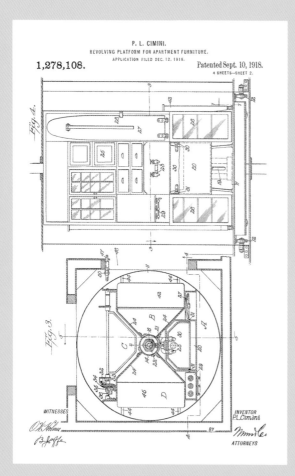

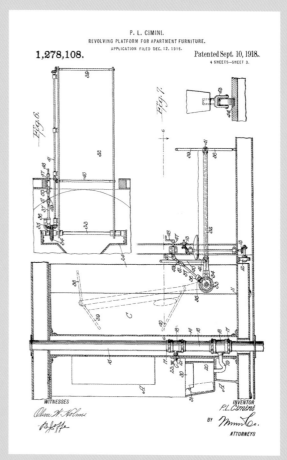

LEFT: Pasquale Cimini's patent showing layout of turntable and elevation of kitchen section
RIGHT: Pasquale Cimini's patent showing operation of fold-up bed

to a secret passage. There is also something James Bondian about these gadgety contraptions that converted a single-room apartment into a four-room apartment with the flip of a lever or the turn of a crank. This appeal of push-button technology as a means of instantly remaking one's environment threads its way through the history of rotating design up to present day.

The development of internally rotating residences was not limited to the United States. In 1924 plans circulated for a German apartment unit with a tripartite turntable.[38] The design was proposed as a viable approach to solving housing shortages—in this case, the housing crisis that arose in Germany after World War I. According to newspaper accounts the apartment was inspired by revolving theater stages developed in Germany several decades before. As with the American internally rotating designs, the apartment consisted of a single room with the turntable in a corner. However, unlike the American patents, the German model had a large turntable with considerable occupiable floor area. One section was fitted out as a living room, complete with divan and grand piano. The second section had a dining table, and the third featured a bed, dressing table, and other bedroom furnishings. When publicized in the United States, a popular youth magazine wrote dismissively of the idea, "occupying a cell shaped like a piece of pie doesn't strike us as an especially attractive proposition. 'Compartment house' would be a good name for the new architectural horror."[39]

This reaction was clearly shared by others, as the concept failed to win even modest popularity during this period. Internally rotating homes would present interpersonal challenges perhaps unique in the history of cohabitation. The concept might work well enough for a single occupant, but could quickly break down when multiple roommates try to share a space in which only one activity can effectively occur at a time. Patents and newspaper articles did not mention what happened when one resident wanted to use the main room as a bedroom while the other wanted to eat there. Technological challenges may also have played a role in the failure of internally rotating houses. Incorporating sinks, stoves, toilets, and electrical outlets into platforms that turned was possible, but not easy. Without them the benefits of a rotating design were only partially fulfilled; with them it was a much more complicated and expensive project. The prospect of maintaining these systems along with their ball-bearing tracks, motors, gears, and retractable furnishings must have further reduced the concept's appeal.

Externally Rotating Houses

While internally rotating designs focus inward to improve spatial qualities and efficiencies, externally rotating houses mediate between the structure's inhabitants and the world outside. During the first half of the twentieth century there were two main motives for rotating an entire house. One goal was to control at will the position of the structure relative to the sun and the wind, whether for health or comfort. The amount of sunlight or breeze a particular area of the house received throughout the day became a negotiable sum. A second objective was to expand the range of views available to the occupant. Rotating houses broke free from the standard house configuration where the scene visible through any particular window generally remained fixed throughout the life of the structure. They capitalized, in many cases quite literally, on dramatic sites and accommodated neatly the rising cultural and economic importance of the view.

Among the earliest twentieth-century designs for an externally rotating residence was Thomas Gaynor's 1908 Rotary Building. Patented but apparently never built, the house featured an entirely conventional exterior indistinguishable from stationary houses. Working at a time before modernism had challenged traditional building forms, it is likely Gaynor intentionally adopted an unexceptional exterior to make his idea appear less radical. Later, externally rotating house designers expanded the vocabulary of exterior forms and features, employing those that suggested a building's kinetic abilities and fully took advantage of their mobility.

As with internally rotating houses during this period, designers were much more common than builders. Newspaper and magazine articles discuss plans for the impending construction of houses that remained unrealized, both by established designers such as the Italian architect Pier Luigi Nervi (designed in 1932) and amateurs articulating personal visions. These plans often revealed a desire to translate professional successes and the power that accompanied them to the built world. For example, in 1908 Manhattan jewelry magnate William Reiman developed, with the help of architect Clarence True, a new design for his own residence. Reiman wanted a house

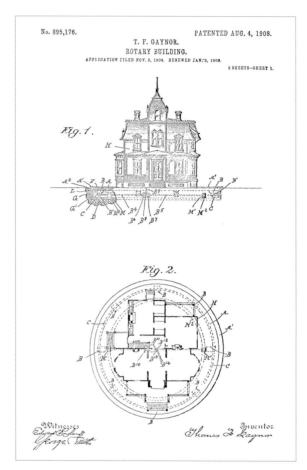

that offered him full control of his environment, from the view to the amount of daylight and air circulation.

Working the remote controls, his whims were to be satisfied with the whir of an electric motor and the quiet churning of gears. One account described Reiman's all-powerful vision: "the owner, in his library or bedroom, may press a button, and on the piazzas will sound a tinkling of bells to those who are about to enter or leave the house, warning

Thomas Gaynor's patent for a rotating house, 1908

them that the Reiman home is about to manoeuvre by either the right or left flank." "Of course sunlight and shade will be his to command, and if he desires to sleep late and light is in his window, he presses the button near his bed and swings away from the east."[40] Though construction was expected to be completed on a site at Bayside, Long Island, within the year, there is no evidence that the house was ever built.

Another well-publicized design that remained unrealized was by Polish-born concert pianist and part-time innovator Józef Hofmann. Hofmann typifies the independent inventor who took up revolving designs during the period; his other creations included pneumatic shock absorbers, windshield wipers, and numerous medical devices. His design, intended for property in South Carolina, had three control panels, one for him, one for his wife, and one in a central control room. Yet he still saw it as a tool for he alone to dominate the environment: "I admit…that this whole idea of the revolving house, as I have planned it, is an autocratic scheme. It is arranged so that the heads of the house may have exactly the conditions they like and the rest of the household must accept this arrangement."[41]

Externally rotating house designs can be seen as a continuation of human efforts to harness the natural world. Earlier in the nineteenth century, wilderness was tamed with mills, canals, railroads, and steamships— technology and machinery were the tools of both a physical transformation and a psychological shift that acknowledged a new era of human influence on their surroundings.

As one historian of technology put it, "they believed that creative minds inventing and controlling machines could transform nature by organizing it for human ends."[42] Turning a house to fill a room with daylight or provide cooling shade, refreshing breeze, or protection from cold winds created the perception that the owner commanded the sun and weather.

Villa Girasole

"I have decided to make the complete turn."[43] Euphoric over seeing his still-under-construction house rotate its planned 180 degrees for the first time, the Italian civil engineer Angelo Invernizzi quickly wrote a colleague that the final version had to go all the way around. It was called the Villa Girasole, a summer house set on a hillside of vineyards and orchards above his home village Marcellise, near Verona. Girasole was the first well-known, built rotating house. It was an experiment, a showpiece, and a unique personal statement that resulted from the collaborative efforts of several designers.

Born in 1884, Invernizzi attended university in Genoa and worked for the state railway in Padua. After graduation he did technical drawings for the railroad for several years. His daughter Lidia is certain it was there, immersed in the technology of transportation, that her father first developed the idea of a rotating house.[44] After World War I Invernizzi established his own firm in Genoa and developed an expertise in reinforced concrete construction. While he may have ruminated on the idea for years, the first drawings of his rotating villa date to 1929.

Villa Girasole from the air, with the courtyard of
the rotating section facing uphill, 1935

OPPOSITE
Villa Girasole's structural frame

THIS PAGE
LEFT: Villa Girasole's podium hall looking
toward central shaft with circular stair
and elevator RIGHT: Spiral staircase wrapping
around the elevator

Angelo Invernizzi's study in the rotating section

Building began in 1931, and proceeding only during the summer months, was completed in 1935.

Invernizzi and his design team used the villa project as a laboratory for trying out modern materials, from reinforced concrete to fiber-cement wall boards. In keeping with the project's experimental nature, a considerable amount of adaptation and refinement accompanied construction. On the exterior walls Invernizzi substituted aluminum sheet for the original cement finish when cracks appeared after the first trial rotations. As the foundation settled and the rotating mechanism was tested, small cracks also developed along the interior plaster walls of the moving part. Invernizzi concealed the damage by finishing the walls with a canvas covering, which provided a textural, handcrafted counterpoint to the sleek exterior skin.

To move through the house is to experience a series of transitions, from heavy to light, from dim to bright, from ceremonial and public to intimate and private, and from traditional to modern. Through the entry at the base of the monumental stucco podium is a hallway that burrows into the hillside. Approaching the tower base, the hall gradually fills with sunlight bounced from the windows and glass tiles far above. A spiral staircase twists along the tower wall, snaking around an open cage elevator that makes quick work of the distance between the podium's lower floor and the moving part's upper level. On the first floor of the V-shaped moving part, the environment changes to one more intimate and informal. This floor is the "day zone," with a dining room on the end of one wing and a music room at the other. In

between are Mr. and Mrs. Invernizzi's studies and a smoking room. Service rooms including the kitchen, pantry, cloakroom, and toilet are tucked into corners near the tower. The second floor features a series of bedrooms and bathrooms arranged symmetrically along each wing.

The layout and form of the moving section are well suited to rotation. Originally, the floor plan of each wing had rooms on both sides of a central hallway. Before construction, however, the design was revised to have the main hallways extend from the central tower along the outer edges so that all the main living rooms and bedrooms would face the terrace enclosed by the wings. Though the views from either wing differ at any given moment, they share a general orientation to the sun, reducing the chance for conflict over which direction the house should point. All rooms could share an equal amount of daylight or shade. Occupants control rotation using a panel (with three buttons: forward, backward, and stop) in the foyer of the moving part. Its single speed was approximately nine inches per minute or one complete rotation in nine hours and twenty minutes.

The transition between classical and contemporary experienced inside is especially notable on the exterior. The stationary podium is monumental and heavy. Above, the mobile wings are light, smooth, and evocative of both art deco and the International Style. The effect is similar to that seen in Jean Saidman's revolving solaria, the first of which predated Girasole by only a few years. In part, the duality of Girasole's exterior is attributable to the collaborative design process, which included Invernizzi and his friend

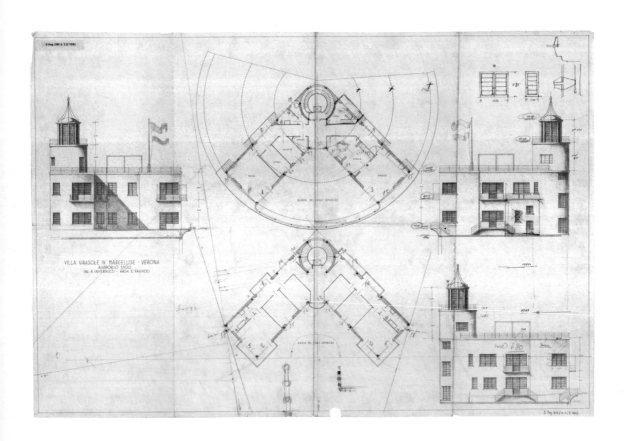

Villa Girasole first- and second-floor plans and
elevations before Invernizzi decided to have the
house rotate 360 degrees

LEFT: Villa Girasole, first-floor hall in rotating section, 2006 RIGHT: Dining room, first floor of rotating section, 2006

and colleague, architect Ettore Fagiuoli, as well as a mechanical engineer and interior designer. Architects and theorists David Lewis, Marc Tsurumaki, and Paul Lewis liken the design to the results of a round of "exquisite corpse," the 1920s surrealist parlor game in which successive participants drew part of a figure, folded the paper to conceal all but the edge of their drawing, and passed it on to the next contributor until the subject was complete and the paper unfurled to reveal "an unanticipated whole" in which "the end result is more than the cumulative product of individual contributions."[45]

A young girl when the house was completed, Lidia Invernizzi recently recalled the thrill of spending summers in this retreat, which also featured a concrete swimming pool and tennis court. Dances were held regularly in the piano room. The garden and countryside provided a bounty of fruits and vegetables that were enjoyed throughout the season and picked and packed for the winter spent in Genoa. Of course, the main attraction was the house's ability to turn. During those first summers, Girasole was rotated daily, out of sheer novelty and for the benefit of frequent visitors. Angelo Invernizzi appreciated most the view provided by the promontory-like terrace. More than half a century later, his daughter recalled, "I remember my father sitting next to the edge of the terrace looking at the landscape, staying there for hours, very relaxed and peaceful."[46]

During World War II, German and then British troops occupied the house. When the Invernizzis returned they found it dirty but intact; only two armchairs were missing. Mrs. Invernizzi died at the villa in 1957, as did her

husband the following year. In the decades that followed, their children continued to use and maintain the home.

The Villa Girasole is one of the few rotating structures to find a place in published histories of architecture, and scholars have made considerable efforts to fit this peculiar design into established narratives of the past. With an aluminum skin, wrap-around windows, and wheels beneath, the rotating part of Villa Girasole suggested a clean break with traditional architectural forms and an embrace of mobility, dynamism, and the machine—tenets shared by futurism, an artistic movement then percolating through interwar Italy. It has also been presented as an artifact of Mussolini's Italy. In the 1930s and '40s the Fascist government espoused a "cult of sun" ideology that considered solar radiation a source not only of health and hygiene, but also of a uniquely Mediterranean vitality and virility. This outlook found expression in a variety of projects, including experimental solar heating systems and urban and architectural designs adapted to the sun's trajectory. Heliocentrism was accompanied by a veneration of machinery and technology. In these contexts moveable architecture, and the rotating house in particular, was seen not as an eccentric folly, but a timely, practical, and rational means of applying technology to the utilization of natural resources.[47] Some writers consider the house so determinedly rational, so excessively dedicated to "heliotropic speculation," that the result is "a villa bordering on the edge of the irrational."[48]

The sun was obviously a prominent theme in the house's design—its rays were featured in a stylized graphic of the house

reproduced in a tile floor mosaic and custom-made dinnerware, and it is embodied in the very name of the house, "The Sunflower" in English. But in contrast to the flower that moved to follow the sun across the sky, the Villa Girasole was often turned to limit rather than maximize exposure to the sun. Lidia Invernizzi noted that the house was designed to be occupied only during the summer months. Typically during hot summer days the moving part of the house was oriented to the north, shading the rooms from direct sunlight.[49]

Invernizzi's design should be seen equally as a means of structuring and controlling the relationship to the surrounding landscape. With its overall height and its positioning far up the hillside, Girasole is a platform upon which the vineyards, orchards, and valleys can be regarded from a distance; the landscape is an inaccessible vista. But when the house is turned so that the terrace faces uphill, the rooms are enclosed by a topography that is immediate and secluded. When the house is oriented in this direction, the central terrace is linked to a landing constructed on the hillside, enabling one to walk directly from the house into the garden. The building and the landscape that surround it are experienced in different ways depending upon the orientation of the former to the latter. The experience of the landscape and the Girasole's relationship to it is totally up to the whim of the person at the controls.

The Villa Girasole cannot be accurately considered without placing it in the broader context of popular (and political) interest in movement and motion, technology, and the machine that was so prevalent at the time of

OPPOSITE
TOP: Villa Girasole's roller-bearing assembly at the bottom of the central column
BOTTOM: Girasole's railcar bogies

THIS PAGE
Villa Girasole's logo

its construction. The house is steeped in these concepts, above and beyond the simple fact that it turns. The mobile portion is clad in an aluminum alloy manufactured by a Milanese company that specialized in aircraft, railroad, and nautical markets. The fifteen sets of wheels beneath the moving wings are adapted railcar bogies; the rest of the rotational machinery uses the same technology as railroad turntables. The wheels were designed to be plainly visible from the exterior, both to simplify maintenance and, no doubt, to further accentuate the villa's mobility. Its interior decoration and custom-designed furnishings incorporated the curving lines of art deco motifs, forms common to 1930s airport designs. Balcony railings, rooftop sun decks, and exterior stairways resemble those found on steamships.

Rotating Amusements

Thomas Gaynor's 1904 patent application for his rotating house suggested that its turntable and machinery could also be used for a spherical amusement attraction decorated on the exterior to resemble a globe. It was an idea probably inspired by the Celestial Globe, an exhibit at the 1900 Paris Universal Exposition.⁵⁰ Inside, four wedge-shaped elevator cabs with stepped seating sections traveled up a stationary central core. Interior floor levels, rotating as part of the turntable, presented different moving tableaux to the audience in the elevators. On the central floor, the passengers could briefly disembark for refreshments and a view out portholes. The design was a buckshot approach to the development of rotating structures, in which Gaynor fired off multiple proposals in the hope that at least one would attract licensees. Though never built, his globe proposal also illustrates the continuing allure of monumental revolving amusement rides. Into the twentieth century seaside resort piers and boardwalks like Blackpool in Great Britain and Coney Island and Atlantic City in the United States offered ever more exciting rides and attractions. International expositions and fairs continued to feature tall signature structures (following the lead of the Eiffel Tower and the Ferris wheel) that offered patrons a once-in-a-lifetime experience.

Somewhat similar in concept to Gaynor's sphere, but on an altogether larger scale, was Samuel M. Friede's Globe Tower, proposed for construction on Coney Island. The enormous structure was to be 300 feet in diameter and 700 feet tall, outsizing by far any other attraction on the boardwalk. Announced in 1906, the tower's steel framework was to enclose eleven separate levels, with a vaudeville theater, skating rink, four-ring circus, hotel, ballroom, weather observatory, roller coaster, and several dining establishments.⁵¹ Just below the sphere's equator, a ring of glass windows was to mark the location of a restaurant with, according to one account, "a revolving strip twenty-five feet wide [that] would carry tables, kitchens and patrons around the outer edge of the Tower to give the effect of eating in an airborne dining car."⁵² On top of the globe, the world's largest revolving light would serve as a beacon to ships at sea and pleasure-seekers across the New York area.

But despite two groundbreaking ceremonies in 1906 and 1907 (complete with bands and fireworks), the sale of tens of thousands of dollars of stock, and the purported purchase of 4,000 tons of steel, the Globe Tower never grew above some concrete foundations. Eventually, the tower company's treasurer was arrested and charged with absconding with stock proceeds; in 1908 the owner of the property removed the foundations for the tower that many suspected was never intended to be anything more than an elaborate financial swindle.⁵³

The 1915 Panama-Pacific International Exposition was held in San Francisco to celebrate the completion of the Panama Canal. Situated in the center of the fair a crane-like metal tower called the Aeroscope swept visitors high into the air and gently turned to provide a 360-degree view of the site and city. A rectangular passenger cabin seating 120 passengers was set at the far end of the Aeroscope arm, while a solid concrete slab on the opposite side of the base acted as counterweight. To load and unload passengers the cabin was lowered to the ground. The arm lifted the cabin 260 feet in the air

COPYRIGHTED 1906 BY FRIEDE GLOBE TOWER CO.

FRIEDE GLOBE TOWER
700 FEET HIGH
CONEY ISLAND, NEW YORK

REAR VIEW
of AEROSCOPE
PAN-PAC. INT. EXPOSITION
SAN FRANCISCO, 1915

E 74

LEFT: Samuel L. Friede's Globe Tower design; windows in the center of the sphere were for a revolving restaurant. **RIGHT:** Aeroscope, Panama-Pacific International Exposition, San Francisco, 1915

as the wheeled base, set atop a ground-level circular track, rotated. Author Laura Ingalls Wilder visited the exposition and in a letter home likened the Aeroscope to "some giant with a square head, craning his long neck up and up."[54]

Designed by Joseph Strauss (who was also chief engineer for the Golden Gate Bridge), the Aeroscope was a celebration of the high technology and engineering that made the Panama Canal possible.[55] While some visitors saw it as a neck-craning giant, the Aeroscope also resembled the large rotating steam shovels that carved the canal. Like the 250-foot-tall Ferris wheel at Chicago's Columbian Exposition and Jesse Lake's rotating observation towers, the Aeroscope was a landmark structure that combined height and rotation to present a new perspective on the world below.

Rotating Bars and Restaurants

Legendary syndicated columnist Harlan Miller once described a revolving bar as a place "where one drink made em' as dizzy as two."[56] In the decades before World War II, a number of bars and nightclubs, including Chicago's Morrison Hotel bar, the Chez Ami in Buffalo, New York, and the Carousel in New Orleans, had rotating bars of various configurations. During the Prohibition era, when alcohol was illegal in the United States, rotating bars were built in the more elegant speakeasies that clandestinely catered to a well-heeled clientele willing to pay a dollar a drink (equivalent to fifteen dollars in 2007).

Spectacles in and of themselves, rotating bars were typically designed to be attractions for out-of-towners and leisure seekers. As such they were often found in tourist districts or near recreation sites. In 1935 the Merry-Go-Round nightclub with its outdoor "ship's deck dance floor and revolving bar" opened at Atlantic Beach, Long Island, a popular escape near New York City.[57] Some rotating bars like the Merry-Go-Round and the Top of the Mark on the rooftop of the Mark Hopkins Hotel in San Francisco featured folding or removable walls that could be set aside during warmer weather. This open arrangement heightened the whimsical, carousel-like character of the bars, provided more interesting views to the outside and, when the bar was at ground level, showed off the rotating feature to passersby.

In 1929 Norman Bel Geddes, designer of the *Ladies' Home Journal* house and the rotary airport, developed plans for an Aërial Restaurant intended (but never built) for the 1933 Century of Progress Exposition in Chicago. Bel Geddes was already an established theatrical designer who had recently turned his attention to creating up-to-date appliances, buildings, automobiles, and airplanes. He also patented new spoons, dishes, pin clips, and radio cabinets. Some of his designs made it into production; others were more fanciful proposals that were never built, such as a nine-level transatlantic airplane meant to compete with ocean liners. His work exhibited aerodynamic, stream-lined forms that he further emphasized by using up-to-date materials like aluminum and chrome. The smooth sweeping lines and rounded corners of his houses and other objects looked fast, even if they were never intended to actually move. They were

"BUFFALO'S THEATRE RESTAURANT" CHEZ AMI — HOME OF THE REVOLVING BAR

an eye-pleasing metaphor for the increasingly rapid pace of modern life, optimistic symbols of a future characterized by progress and efficiency.

The Aërial Restaurant consisted of a central steel column carrying three passenger and nine service elevators to a height of 280 feet. There, a three-part structure contained restaurants and observation decks that would provide a sweeping a view of the exposition grounds and the surrounding city and lake. According to Bel Geddes, the structure was meant to first attract local visitors. In his 1932 book *Horizons*, he wrote, "the chief reason that brought about the designing of The Aërial Restaurant was its novelty to first attract a repeat audience of Chicagoans themselves to the exposition grounds."[58]

The upper structure was to be a complex of dining and entertaining establishments. The three separate wedges had arcs ranging from 240 to 180 degrees. Each wedge included an enclosed restaurant, a single story high, with glass walls from floor to ceiling. Doors opened onto an observation terrace around the perimeter. The lowest level included a restaurant seating 700, dance floor, orchestra space, and pantry. On the middle level a cafe and bar seated 500, while the top level had a more exclusive restaurant for 200 diners, where "the best food may be obtained at admittedly high prices."[59]

Postcard showing Chez Ami's rotating bar, ca. 1930s

What Bel Geddes called "the building's greatest novelty," was that the entire upper section with restaurants and observation decks was designed to slowly revolve. Though each of the three levels appeared to be structurally independent, apparently they were to turn in unison. A description of the restaurant's rotating mechanism suggests that at that stage of the process Bel Geddes' design was perhaps not fully considered. According to the book, the machinery was to be located beneath the ground-floor restaurant that serviced the restaurants above.[60] Such an arrangement would have required a complicated drive shaft assembly over twenty stories tall, rather than the much simpler arrangement of locating the rotating motor within the restaurant head, a treatment later universally adopted for similar structures.

Bel Geddes raised his restaurants to a height sufficient to provide a dramatic view while also occupying a minimum footprint on the lot below. Indeed this was one of the selling points of the building, intended for an exposition site that was already crowded with planned structures. Conceived during the Great Depression and undoubtedly exceptionally expensive, the Aërial Restaurant project was never constructed. However, the design for a glass-walled circular restaurant perched atop a slender tower, and its function as a centerpiece of an international exposition, foreshadowed the era of the revolving restaurant three decades in the future.

The first half of the twentieth century saw a lot of drawing and discussion related to revolving architecture, but little construction. Economic and political tumult hindered the realization of some projects. Others were held back by the reservations of clients or a public yet to be convinced of the wisdom of revolving design. Successes came primarily in treatment structures (which antibiotics would soon make wholly obsolete) and theater stages. Those who considered revolving buildings an apt expression of the century's emphasis on mobility and a sensible response to common concerns of the era would have to wait until well into the postwar period. Then, spurred by a sustained economic expansion, structures that turned would begin to be built in substantial numbers, and existing motives—efficiency, convenience—would be joined with new cultural priorities from futuristic theming to urban redevelopment to green design.

OPPOSITE
Model of Norman Bel Geddes' Aërial Restaurant, proposed, but never built, for the 1933 Century of Progress Exposition in Chicago

CHAPTER THREE

POSTWAR ROTATING DESIGNS

......................———————.......

After two decades of depression and war many in the United States and Europe were ready to start anew. By the late 1950s recovery was well underway and more design projects became reality. A postwar economic boom pushed consumer spending to unprecedented levels, expanded the middle class, and spurred the growth of tourism and entertainment industries. Often presented as a break with past "traditional" forms, modernism came to dominate office and institutional design. New ideas for buildings of all sorts were explored to meet a range of postwar imperatives: demand for massive amounts of affordable housing, accommodating the increasingly ubiquitous automobile, supporting new communication networks, and entertaining increasingly prosperous populations in search of exciting experiences. Some saw a prominent place in the postwar world for revolving architecture. When sky-high restaurants set on turntables became an international phenomenon in the 1960s, they encouraged the development of other rotating buildings, and a future filled with revolving architecture seemed within reach.

As America's affection for the automobile grew exponentially in the postwar years, turntables continued to prove a useful means of fitting them into tight spaces. Designs called for inserting drive-through banking services within buildings. In structures like the Farmer's and Mechanic's Bank in Minneapolis, cars entered the ground floor from the street, drove to the teller booth, then proceeded to a turntable at the rear, which rotated to reorient the cars back toward the street. The entire arrangement, woven between structural columns and demanding precise aim on the turntable, was not for squeamish drivers.[1]

Car turntables were also incorporated into plans for multilevel automated parking garages, though it appears they were never built. Designs such as the 1950 Rotogarage by Albert Buranelli had a turntable on each floor with elevators in the center. The car would be raised to a level with an empty space and the turntable rotated so that the space lined up with the elevator entrance. With three concentric, independently rotating, rings rather than a single perimeter ring, plans for the twelve-story Gyro Parking Garage were even more elaborate. These designs boasted double the capacity of regular ramp garages, made possible with turntables and high-tech "electronic memory systems."[2] Rotating garages were akin to internally rotating house designs from earlier in the century. Both reduced unused space by getting

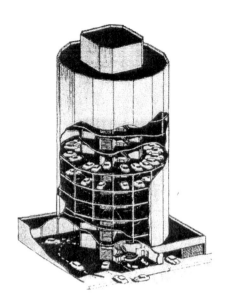

Rotogarage design
by Albert Buranelli,
ca. 1955

could vary the size of the seating area, from expansive to intimate, or could change the position of the stage within the structure, from placing it at one end for a more traditional arrangement to centering it in the middle of the auditorium for an in-the-round configuration. Some of these unbuilt designs called for seating areas that rotated in their entirety and could be turned between acts or in the midst of a performance to change settings or track the actors' movements.

In the late 1940s Norman Bel Geddes called for the development of new forms to replace what he derisively called the "picture frame" stage. Like earlier theater reformers such as Lautenschläger and Reinhardt, Bel Geddes argued that proscenium theaters were "the most limiting form of structure the theatre had ever known," because they separated performers from audience and because they restricted theater to a two- rather than three-dimensional experience. His alternative was the Flexible Theater, in which the stage and seating areas could be rearranged in any number of configurations. Moved between shows, the stage would be positioned in the center, or jut into the audience, or run as a strip with seating on two sides. Such a plastic performance space would spur the creativity of designers, directors, writers, and performers, while breaking down what he saw as a stifling division between audience and action.[4] While the Flexible Theater was never constructed, Bel Geddes' ideas were incorporated into numerous innovative theaters developed in subsequent decades.

The Revolving Auditorium Theatre is an outdoor theater located in the southern

rid of circulation areas (ramps and hallways) in order to maximize the efficiency of limited floor plates.

The development and construction of turntable stages continued in the postwar era. New versions were often fitted to a short "wagon" equipped with casters so that the entire apparatus could be rolled backstage when not in use. The turntable wagon designed for Manhattan's Metropolitan Opera in the late 1960s, for example, had a 57-foot diameter but was only 12 inches high.[3] While these turntables provided quick scenery changes, and were occasionally used for dynamic effects, they still were set within traditional proscenium stage theaters.

In the second half of the twentieth century, designers continued prewar experimentation with theaters in which various components rotated and shifted to reconfigure the space. The operators of such theaters

TOP: Prototype rotating auditorium at Český Krumlov, ca. 1958
LEFT: Soldiers turning the first full-sized revolving auditorium in Český Krumlov, ca. 1965

Czech Republic town of Český Krumlov. Conceived by theater designer Joan Brehms, it consists of a ovoid-shaped, raked seating area set in the gardens of a Baroque 1754 summer palace called Bellarie. The design reflected Brehms's view that "theatre space must be dramatic and dynamic, not decorative, but one compact space at the same time. It must enable a lot of changeable opportunities and variatability during a performance."[5]

In 1958 Brehms developed a scale model of his design, followed by a small prototype platform in the palace garden that accommodated an audience of sixty. The prototype was a success, for the following year the company built a full-scale version seating 400. Also located in the garden, it could be oriented toward Bellarie's facade, as well as the palace gardens, which represented a variety of settings from formal terraced gardens to forests, fields, and bushes in the theater's productions. Photos from the period show the seating platform being rotated mid-performance by a group of recruit soldiers. Two years later the outdoor theater was expanded and improved; a motor was connected to the wheels and the entire facility was made permanent. In 1969 the theater was expanded to include an orchestra space and an enlarged seating area for over 650 spectators, a configuration that survives to the present.

The same year the full-sized Český Krumlov auditorium was constructed, the Pyynikki Open Air Theatre opened in Tampere, Finland. Designed by architect Reijo Ojanen, it was similar to Brehms's version, with a revolving seating area for an audience of 800 that could be turned to face different sets located in the surrounding landscape. In recent years the theater has been expanded, and a roof constructed over the seating area.

The revolving auditoria at Bellarie and Tampere opened new possibilities for directors and designers. Used creatively, these forms introduce a dynamism and engagement with the audience that is markedly different from a conventional theater. The audience becomes more of an active participant than a spectator as the action unfolds literally around them and they turn to face new settings. The experience can also be cinematic. Like a panning shot that seamlessly tracks a film character from one location to another, the theater can be easily turned so that the entire audience follows the actors from one location to the next. The production can be staged to suggest that the settings are at a distance spatially and even temporally.

In 1960 French theoretician and designer Jacques Polieri developed a more elaborate version of these designs with his Théâtre Mobile for the Festival of Avant-Garde Art in Paris. The building included a rotating platform with seating for an audience of three to four hundred set off center within an outer annular rotating stage. Because the components turned independently and off center a variety of effects could be created. As on historian noted, "when moving in a particular configuration, the spectator experienced a sense of telescopic movement—moving closer to an object and then receding, creating an effect something like the 'whip' ride at an amusement park."[6]

An increase in the construction of cultural centers and school auditoria during the postwar era encouraged the development

OPPOSITE
TOP: Open-air Revolving Auditorium in Český Krumlov, ca. 2005
BOTTOM: Pyynikki Open Air Theatre, Tampere, Finland, operating the rotation controls; view from the revolving auditorium showing a performance of the play *The Unknown Soldier*, ca. 1970

Time-lapse image
showing Český
Krumlov's Open-air
Revolving
Auditorium
in motion, ca. 2005

of reconfigurable spaces that could be quickly adapted for small or large events. International expositions also used moveable seating structures to generate interest, efficiently move large crowds, and project a vision of the future. The General Electric Pavilion designed by Welton Becket Associates for the 1964 World's Fair featured a large ringed seating area that carried an audience of 1,400 around six separate stages located in the center of the ring. The Chrysler exhibit at the fair had a similar configuration—an auditorium surrounding

a circular stage—but in this version, the stage (featuring a puppet show) was divided into three sections that presented the performance's acts in succession.[7] It was a single-level version of what Thomas Gaynor envisioned in 1908 for his patented globe attraction.

Revolving Restaurants

One of the most popular pavilions at the 1964 New York World's Fair was the General Motors–sponsored Futurama II. A sequel to the original exhibit (designed by Norman

Bel Geddes for the 1939–40 World's Fair), it featured rows of seats set on tracks winding through an enormous diorama that depicted life in 2024. Exuding corporate optimism, the model showed a new age of exploration with lunar and undersea bases, road construction, and a city of the future. The visitor looked down on these miniature worlds of shiny new architecture and ribbons of highway made possible by high technology.

The towering perspective was a contemporary counterpart to that provided by past exposition structures that offered visions of a remade landscape below. By the mid-1960s a new type of permanent attraction was appearing in city centers and on mountain peaks throughout the world that promised a similar experience.

Panoramas of the nineteenth century presented the world as a spectacle that could be viewed anew—from new heights, new angles, even different periods of time. Eiffel's tower provided the opportunity for formal dining high above Paris. It opened to a broader public the aerial perspective that was once exclusive to the balloonist. Jesse Lake's towers and the Aeroscope furthered the introduction of high-altitude vistas to the public. With their rotating mechanisms, they became the real-life counterpart to the moving panorama. Rotating bars provided the chance to drink and socialize while in cyclical motion. During the decades after World War II, entrepreneurs, architects, and engineers combined these various concepts (often unaware of the earlier designs), filtering them though postwar trends in futuristic design, themed entertainment, and the

technical necessities of modern communication infrastructure. The result, revolving restaurants, rapidly spread around the world.

In many countries commercial jet travel, highway construction, and an expanding middle class with disposable income and free time fueled an explosive growth in tourism. In both the Eastern Bloc and the West, the Space Race heightened popular interest in a technological future, while the Cold War fostered both the need for politicized symbols of progress and concerns about the ominous downsides of technology. World's fairs, international expositions, and Olympic games called for updated signature structures to rival those of the past. Phone and television companies built tall towers for broadcasting and relaying signals, towers that offered platforms for additional revenue-generating enterprises. Revolving restaurants fit the needs of civic boosters and politicians seeking signs of status, entrepreneurs hoping to attract customers, and a public impatient for life in the future.

One of the first postwar revolving restaurants was a modest cafe called the Merry-Go-Round, opposite the University of Miami campus. With a structure featuring six booths, decorated with bird cutouts, arranged around a pipe organ and covered with a tent-like top, its carousel theme was hard to miss. Clearly a descendant of the rotating bars built during the first half of the twentieth century (many of which were merry-go-round themed), it bore little resemblance to the sleek revolving restaurants that appeared on rooftops, tower tops, and mountain tops in the decades that followed.

Merry-Go-Round
Cafe at the
University of Miami,
1955 postcard

A Start in Germany

For thousands of years tall towers—pagodas, minarets, cathedral bell towers, and castle towers—have expressed spiritual beliefs, aided defense, and demonstrated power and prestige. Ever thinner and higher, they flaunted technical ability. As status symbols they added to the beauty and renown of a structure or town. They reflected ambition, authority, and, more recently, modernity. Historian Anton Huurdeman has noted that "in the nineteenth century, high chimneys in the landscape were appreciated as symbols of industrial progress. Similarly, in the twentieth century, telecommunications towers became visible signs of the information society."[8]

New microwave communication systems introduced in the 1950s required a series of transmitters linked by line-of-sight. At the time most towers were steel lattice frames. When a basic steel tower was planned for a prominent hilltop in Stuttgart, West Germany, a structural engineer named Fritz

Leonhardt convinced government authorities to go with a more elegant form made of reinforced concrete. When it was completed in 1956, the Stuttgart Tower was the first reinforced concrete TV tower in the world.

To help defray building and operating costs, Leonhardt and his collaborator, architect Erwin Heinle, proposed that the tower design be expanded to include tourist attractions along with the broadcasting equipment housed in the head structure perched at the top of the shaft. At a height of over 450 feet, the final cylindrical head design included two observation decks and a stationary restaurant overlooking the city and its surrounding hills, vineyards, and forests. An antenna mast continued above the head, narrowing to a point and lending the structure an appearance similar to an olive skewered on a toothpick. Both this tapered concrete shaft-head-mast configuration and the inclusion of observation and dining facilities within the head were repeated in many of the towers that followed.

Three years later, a second concrete TV tower was built in West Germany, based loosely on the Stuttgart design. The opening of Dortmund's Florianturm coincided with a national horticultural fair on the grounds surrounding the tower. The tower featured an upper and lower head, the latter with what may have been the first revolving restaurant ever built in a tower. A stationary core in the center of the lower head accommodated the stairs and elevators continuing up from the shaft as well as restrooms and food preparation space. Revolving around this service core was a turntable floor that carried the tables, chairs, and diners on a once-every-hour circuit of the view.

The work of Leonhardt and his colleagues put West Germany at the forefront of reinforced concrete tower design. They honed the process of slipform construction, in which an assembly of hydraulic jacks placed along the shaft continually pushes upward the formwork used to contain and shape each successive layer of concrete. They were the first to run elevators along the outside of the shaft, and they explored a variety of different head and shaft configurations, always working to balance aesthetics and efficiency. As functional engineered structures, the towers exhibited a clean simplicity and purity of form made possible by the creative use of reinforced concrete.[9]

Also in the late 1950s construction began on two other revolving restaurants in structures quite different from the TV towers. The concrete Henninger Turm in Frankfurt, Germany, served as a silo complex storing 16,000 tons of barley for a local brewery. To convert a potential public eyesore to a landmark structure that generated additional income, the designers decided to add rooftop amenities. The completed structure included a fully enclosed three-story head with two revolving restaurants (at over 330 feet) and an observation gallery. The entire head structure revolved on the exterior, drawing attention to the accompanying sign and announcing its unique capability to all points below. Henninger Turm opened in May 1961.

In 1958 Harry Hammon and his sister Isobel Fahey purchased an old funicular railway in Katoomba, Australia, originally used

Henninger Turm, with a revolving restaurant in the head, ca. 1965 postcard

for mining operations. They made improvements to the railway, constructing a new aerial cableway and a building that housed a gift shop and coin-operated amusements. Called Scenic World, the attraction's location and rides offered tourists the opportunity to experience the surrounding Blue Mountains as a collection of successive views. The following year they built a square restaurant building with floor-to-ceiling windows that continued this sense of passage through the landscape. The interior dining room has a center-mounted turntable fifty feet in diameter that accommodated 200. Kitchen, restrooms, and other service spaces are located in stationary parts of the building where they would not obstruct the view and

would not require rotating connections and fittings. When the restaurant first opened, the floor turned at a zippy six revolutions per hour, though later it was reduced to three.[10] While in the decades ahead, revolving restaurants with full-disk turntables would be less common than those that used ring turntables, Scenic World's restaurant was an early example of the construction of such facilities overlooking natural wonders and a confirmation of their ability to turn views into profits.

It is not known whether the Seattle architect John Graham Jr. or his associates were aware of the German and Australian revolving restaurants when in 1959 he proposed that the rooftop restaurant his firm was designing for a new Honolulu shopping center be made

to rotate. The concept was clearly novel to his clients, who reportedly answered his presentation with a mix of excitement and disbelief, "can you do that?"[11] One of Graham's designers, John Ridley, developed the rough plans for the rooftop restaurant, and another, Jim Jackson, first suggested that it turn to provide each table a slowly moving 360 degree view of the Waianae Mountains, Diamond Head, and Waikiki Beach.

As the design proceeded and the structure below was changed to a twenty-three-story office building, Graham's Seattle office, John Graham and Company, developed a system similar to that used in Dortmund's Florianturm, in which the glass exterior walls remained fixed and a ring-shaped interior dining area holding 162 diners rotated the tables around the view. Also like the Florianturm, this 16-foot-wide turntable encircled a static core containing space for elevators, restrooms, and food preparation.[12] La Ronde opened in November 1961. Perched like a flying saucer on the otherwise conventionally modern Ala Moana Office Building, it announced a novel attraction for booming Hawaii, and helped usher in an age of revolving architecture.[13]

Until then John Graham Jr. was best known as the designer of retail centers including Seattle's Northgate (1950), considered a prototype for postwar shopping malls. During his architecture studies at Yale, he had heard Buckminster Fuller discuss the round,

Postcard for the Skyway Restaurant in Katoomba, Australia, ca. 1967

metal Dymaxion House. In the early 1960s
the growing popular interest in space-age
design and the coming of an international
exposition provided Graham an opportunity
to develop a structure that was as futuristic
as anything imagined by Fuller.

Space Needle
The Century 21 Exposition was conceived
in the mid-1950s as a way to celebrate the
growth of the Pacific Northwest and respond
to the growing technological prowess on the
other side of the Iron Curtain (confirmed by
the 1957 launch of Sputnik). It was to reflect
the increasing importance of technology to
daily life and, like past World's Fairs, was an

opportunity for the host city, Seattle, to
boost its international prominence. Edward
E. Carlson, president of Western Hotels, led a
coalition of civic leaders, planners, sponsors,
and designers to organize the fair, which was
dedicated to "New Science and the Pan-
Pacific World."

During a 1959 trip to Germany, Carlson
visited Stuttgart's new television tower and
restaurant and returned to the United States
convinced that a tall signature tower was a
necessary addition to the Seattle exposition.
John Graham's office was already working
on a design that would serve as a focal point
for the fair, but its final form was still unde-
termined when Carlson returned. Early
versions were cabled balloon-like structures
and "space-cage" platforms, some raised atop
100-foot legs straddling pools and fountains.
Through several iterations, with contributions by Victor Steinbrueck of the University
of Washington, John Ridley, Art Edwards,
and others in Graham's office, the concept
grew in height and the head structure grew
more slender and simplified in its program.
The designers dropped proposals to include a
full-sized planetarium in the head as Graham
encouraged them to "keep it saucer-like."[14]
Construction began in April 1961 with a
foundation pour that required 467 truckloads
of concrete. Over the next year ironworkers
assembled 147,000 pounds of steel in strong
winds and biting winter cold.

The Eye of the Needle restaurant was
located at 630 feet, in the lower deck of
the tower head. Its turntable, moving so
steadily that "it won't even ripple a martini,"
originally accommodated 250 diners in

Early proposal for Space Needle tower
and landscape, 1960

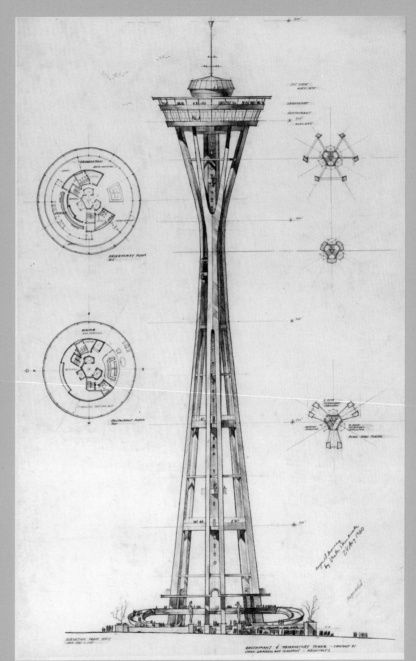

Preliminary drawing of the Space Needle by Victor Steinbrueck, August 1960; while the supporting tower appears close to its final design here, the head structure would be further refined.

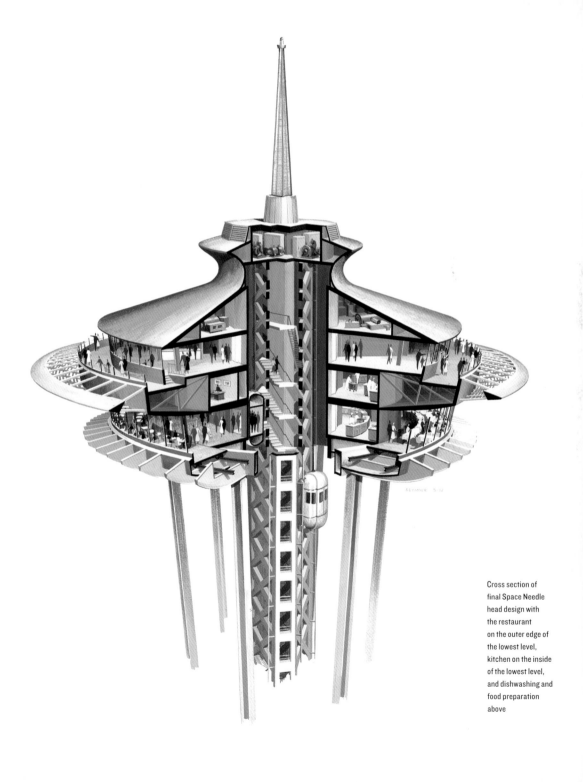

Cross section of
final Space Needle
head design with
the restaurant
on the outer edge of
the lowest level,
kitchen on the inside
of the lowest level,
and dishwashing and
food preparation
above

LEFT: Building the head structure, October 1961
TOP RIGHT: Work underway on the revolving restaurant level, December 1961 **BOTTOM RIGHT:** Completed Eye of the Needle restaurant atop the Space Needle, April 1962

booths and modern pipe-frame chairs overlooking canted windows of tinted glass.[15] The fixed center has a kitchen and foyer where the elevator cabs arrive, and the level above the restaurant features an open-air observation deck and gift shop. On the exterior ringed louvers shade the windows while below, radial steel outriggers extend beyond the head's wall. Together they make up an iconic futuristic design feature that referenced Saturn's rings and the rows of disks commonly found at the end of sci-fi ray guns.

The Needle was a powerful expression of the fair's theme: "Man in the Space Age." Alongside other attractions—a satellite tracking station, arcades that had pinball machines with lunar themes, a "spacearium"—the tower and restaurant presented a vision of future prosperity engendered by a marriage of capitalism and high technology and extending far beyond the earth. While the vocabulary employed was reflective of its own time, the final design for the Space Needle still gave a nod to a famous earlier tower. With its steel legs sweeping upward to meet a central latticework shaft, the Space Needle was in form and function an updated version of Gustave Eiffel's 1887 Parisian masterpiece.

The Space Needle and Eye of the Needle restaurant were completed just before the fair opened in April 1962. Despite waits that often exceeded two hours, tens of thousands visited the observation deck and restaurant during the fair. The Space Needle was publicized in innumerable articles around the world. Elvis Presley and his date dined there in the 1963 film *It Happened at the World's Fair*. The structure became a permanent icon for the city and helped set the stage for the

Interior of Eye of the Needle restaurant, ca. 1962 postcard

proliferation of revolving restaurants across the globe in the 1960s and '70s. Its distinctive profile also established a modern model for many that followed. From the 1976 CN Tower in Toronto to the 1996 Stratosphere Las Vegas and China's 2001 Macau Tower, the tripod legs sweeping toward the center and then curving back outward emphasize both the head and the upward thrust of the tower. The design is gracefully evocative of contrails and the aerodynamic forms of a jet aircraft.

The idea of a high-altitude revolving restaurant spread quickly beyond West Germany, Australia, Honolulu, and Seattle. The success of the early German towers as tourist attractions helped prompt a wave of tower-top revolving restaurant construction in Europe and around the world that continued for decades. Throughout the period numerous projects followed the Ala Moana model, placing revolving restaurants atop hotels, office buildings, and industrial structures. Where, as in Katoomba, Australia, mountain peaks provided dramatic views, entrepreneurs built self-contained revolving restaurants to capitalize on the sights and provide destinations for new cable ways. The Florianturm, Skyview, Henninger Turm, Ala Moana, and Space Needle, all in operation by 1962, served as templates for the hundreds of revolving restaurants that followed. In time a general typology evolved that has remained surprisingly consistent.

Toward a Revolving Restaurant Typology

Most rotating restaurants are like architectural barnacles. They rely on other "host" buildings or natural features to provide the necessary height, concentration of visitors, and a share of the design statement. The host structure or site usually has one of three primary forms: vertical cantilevered towers (the superstars of the genre); commercial and industrial buildings; or mountain tops. Towers built adjacent to tourist-frequented natural wonders like Niagara Falls or as part of fairs or expositions like the Tower of the Americas in San Antonio, Texas, served primarily as observation deck, restaurant attraction, and instant landmark. Other towers were first and foremost telecommunication platforms—revolving restaurants and observation decks were ancillary income generators.

Spawned by the early German television towers and the Space Needle, self-supporting towers were mostly reinforced concrete shafts, round or with radial ribs that usually tapered as they rose upward. Bases had either splayed legs, were concealed within ground-level support structures, or were set entirely below grade. The cores contained staircases,

elevators, and all the necessary cables, pipes, and ductwork. Toward the top of the towers, heads provided space for a combination of transmitters, microwave receivers, and other electronic equipment, as well as observation galleries, offices, kitchens, and restaurants. Heads assumed various shapes—spheres, barrels, disks—with straight or canted walls. Some designs featured multiple heads.

During the 1960s much of the new tower and restaurant construction occurred in Europe. Vienna, Austria's Donauturm (Danube Tower), with two revolving restaurants in the head, was completed in 1964. Moscow's 1,700-foot-tall Ostankino Tower was completed three years later. In Hamburg, Germany's Heinrich-Hertz-Turm opened in 1968, as did Munich's Olympiaturm, which would be a centerpiece of the Olympic complex four years later. In North America, Skylon Tower and its restaurant were built at Niagara Falls in 1965, Calgary Tower in 1967. The Tower of the Americas was built for the 1968 World's Fair in San Antonio. During the 1970s and '80s at least a dozen more towers and accompanying revolving restaurants were built worldwide, with many of the more recent towers appearing in the Middle East and Asia.

While tower restaurants were especially dramatic, those located on building rooftops were more common. Host buildings were typically associated with the tourism industry. Hotels, convention centers, and the occasional shopping center used revolving restaurants as a complement to their other businesses. Marriott, Radisson, and Holiday Inn all built hotels with revolving restaurants. Architect and developer John Portman won

TOP LEFT: Scale model of Donauturm at groundbreaking **TOP RIGHT:** Donauturm design and construction team on the turntable frame, 1964 **BOTTOM LEFT:** Outer ring of wheels below the restaurant deck, Donauturm, 1964 **BOTTOM RIGHT:** Donauturm, opening day, 1964

LEFT: Ostankino Television Tower in Moscow Russia, 2006 BOTTOM: Olympiaturm in Olympiapark, Munich, Germany, framed by a tensile roofing structure used on the stadium and other structures

over the Hyatt chain with his 1967 design for the Hyatt Regency Atlanta. For this project, he put together an influential architectural ensemble that helped resuscitate the urban hotel and attract tourists and locals back to new downtown developments. The design's carved-out interior formed a spacious enclosed atrium. Glass walled elevators ran up the sides of the atrium connecting the ground floor with a dramatic flying-saucer-shaped revolving restaurant set on the rooftop. Portman recently recalled,

> From the beginning, our primary focus was to create space people would enjoy. Our goal was an extraordinary hotel environment that resulted in high occupancy. To add to the marketability of the hotel, we wanted to increase local patronage of the restaurants. Therefore, it made sense to make the rooftop restaurant a destination unto itself. The glass-cabbed ride through the atrium was the first step. Next was for guests to view the city from a new perspective as Atlanta's first revolving restaurant made its 360 degree rotation.[16]

Hyatt and other hotel operators around the world repeated variations on Portman's atrium and restaurant design in the succeeding decades. Revolving restaurants were also built on commercial office buildings and, in one exceptional case, on the roof of a 600-bed dormitory at the University of South Carolina in Columbia.[17]

In successful designs the revolving restaurant fit with the host structure to form a cohesive aesthetic statement. As in the 1976 Harbour Centre Tower in Vancouver, British Columbia, the disk-shaped restaurant might be centered on a rooftop with a symmetrical facade below, related and complementary in scale and massing. Here, the restaurant calls attention to itself, advertising its presence to potential patrons below, but retains a congruence with the host building. Other designs set the revolving restaurant within the structure with an arcing bump out to signal the restaurant's location to viewers on the ground and provide a broad field of view for those within.

Cylindrical hotel and office buildings commonly featured an integrated revolving restaurant discernible from the exterior only through minor changes in the framing or glazing. Buildings like John Portman's seventy-story Westin Peachtree Plaza in Atlanta (1976) had a restaurant at the top. Malaysia's Menara Tun Mustapha building from the following year employed a less conventional treatment, with its Atmosphere restaurant located at the building's midpoint. While the result was a more seamless expression than the typical rooftop pod configuration, such designs sacrificed the important opportunity to highlight and promote the restaurant on the exterior.

The structures beneath revolving restaurants were not exclusively TV towers, hotels, or offices. In fact, the only real requirements of a host building were that it be of sufficient height to offer a view and be publicly accessible. Like Henninger Turm, the Prima Tower restaurant (1977) in Singapore was built atop concrete grain silos near the port. In Reykjavík, Iceland, the Perlan (Pearl) revolving restaurant sits on six enormous tanks used to store geothermal spring water. Set within an enormous glass dome, the

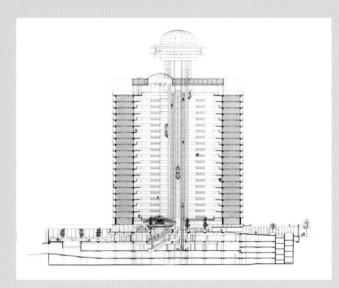

RIGHT: Harbour Centre Tower in Vancouver with a revolving restaurant head structure as a central component of the building
FAR RIGHT: Hong Kong's Furama Hotel's revolving restaurant, La Ronda, set within the upper floor with a curving bump
BOTTOM: Menara Tun Mustapha building, a thirty-story cylindrical tower in Kota Kinabalu, Malaysia, with a revolving restaurant located midway up the building

Perlan's elegant form manages to appropriate the utilitarian water-work structure below. Revolving restaurants in Saudi Arabia and Kuwait were also incorporated into water tower structures. Like an ornate glass collar, the 1998 Beitou Revolving Restaurant in Taipei, Taiwan, wraps around the chimney of a trash incinerator. The restaurant is part of a larger complex that includes a playground, swimming pool, and ash weighing bridge.

Self-contained mountaintop revolving restaurants rely on topography rather than host structures to provide a suitable and profitable perspective. One- or two-story structures, devoted exclusively to serving the tourist market, they are the descendents of nineteenth-century observation points with restaurants and hotels often reached by funicular railways.[18] Like urban cable car companies that built end-of-the-line amusement parks to encourage weekend use, aerial cableway entrepreneurs developed mountaintop destinations to generate traffic and subsidize construction of the cableway. A growing number of these destinations, in the Alps and around the world, eventually featured revolving restaurants.

The view from the mountaintop restaurants was different from that seen from rooftops or towers, but the motivation was largely the same—to attract customers with the spectacle of a dramatic "moving" view, while ensuring uninterrupted access to that view over the course of a visit. Although Australia's 1960 Skyway Restaurant appears to have been one of the first, another mountain-top revolving restaurant in Europe received unsurpassed attention and renown almost a decade later.

TOP: The Pearlan restaurant in Reykjavík, Iceland, sits atop geothermal tanks, 2004. BOTTOM: Interior of the Pearlan restaurant, 2004

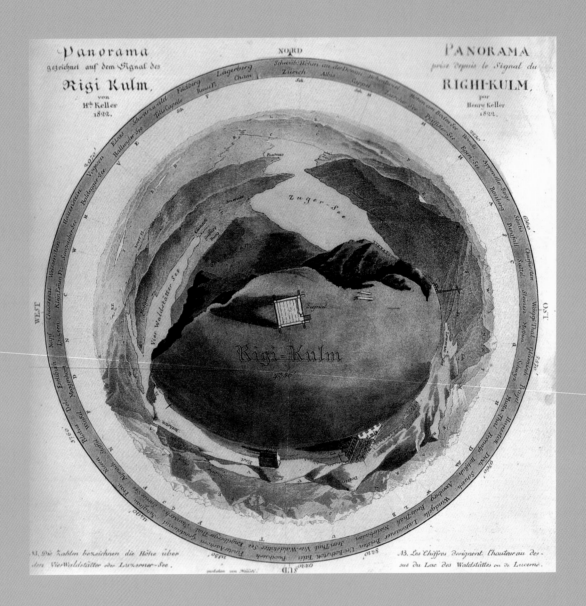

1840 illustration showing the panoramic views
from the Hotel Rigi Kulm in the Swiss Alps

In Switzerland's Bernese Oberland region a 9,748-foot peak called Schilthorn provides an unobstructed view encompassing over 200 other summits. It had long been a popular destination for mountaineers, but various plans developed during the first half of the twentieth century to open the site up to a broader public failed to extend beyond the terminus of a funicular rail service in the mountain village of Mürren. By the late 1950s advances in aerial cableway technology, combined with the increasing use of helicopters to facilitate high-altitude construction, had local entrepreneurs revisiting the goal of building on Schilthorn. Led by Mürren-born businessman Ernst Feuz, a local group secured permission to build a cable network that would reach the peak starting at the valley floor at Stechelberg. Construction began in 1963 and was completed four years later. The total trip to Schilthorn included four changeovers along the way at intermediary stations. Feuz's original sketches of the cableway suggest that he had ideas for the design of each of the stations except for the one at the peak. By the time the cableway was finished, Feuz had developed plans to include a rotating restaurant in the final station.

While the Alps had nearly a dozen mountaintop restaurants by the 1960s, the restaurant at Schilthorn would be the first to rotate.[19] Work progressed slowly but steadily. As with the cableway support towers and two of the intermediary stations at lower altitudes, all materials (concrete, girders, cables) as well as all workers were ferried by helicopter. Crews had to fight areas of deep snow and occasional freezing temperatures even during the summer. Bernese architect

Proposed design for a rotating gondola on the Schilthorn cableway by Raymond Loewy, never built

Konrad Wolfe designed the structure to be prefabricated in sections that could be hoisted to the site and bolted together. Midway through the process, however, construction stalled when Feuz and his partners ran out of money.

At about the same time, in January 1968, Hubert Fröhlich, production manager for the James Bond film *On Her Majesty's Secret Service*, was searching all over the Alps for a real location to match the fictional cableway and peak station described in the Ian Fleming novel on which the film was based. Finally Fröhlich met Ernst Feuz and heard about the Schilthorn project. Within twenty-four hours a contract was in place that allowed the production to film at the restaurant in exchange for financial assistance in completing its construction. Because the interior was yet to be finished, Fröhlich was able to design it to suit

LEFT: James Bond and Bond girls curling on Piz Gloria's terrace
RIGHT: Film producer Albert "Cubby" Broccoli and Ernst Feuz conferring on the Piz Gloria deck, 1968

his needs. The summit building was completed that summer, and filming took place between October and December.

On Her Majesty's Secret Service was the sixth film about the suave British secret agent and the first to star George Lazenby rather than Sean Connery.[20] In the film Bond's nemesis Ernst Blofeld (played by Telly Savalas) attempts to brainwash several women, programming them to disperse mind-controlling chemical agents throughout the world. The entire Schilthorn facility, including the tramway station and what would become the restaurant, served as Piz Gloria, Blofeld's secret laboratory disguised as a health retreat. The exterior was the backdrop for several scenes, including a tense fight among the cables and machinery, a curling competition, and numerous establishing shots with skiers and helicopters. Inside was a large circular room presented in the film as Blofeld's

lounge. Here James Bond, disguised as a Scottish aristocrat, shared dinner and not-so-subtle double entendres with the female "patients" of Blofeld's "clinic."

Made largely of concrete anchored to the rock surface, the terminal station's base features a docking area where cars load and unload, as well as restrooms, offices, and other service areas. Above, a square observation deck wraps around the circular base of the restaurant. The single-story pedestal extends from the center of the main observation deck to support the polygonal restaurant. Its exterior walls were originally made of aluminum-clad spandrels and glass, and a large conical roof with generous eaves topped the building. A walkway connected the restaurant and deck with an adjacent heliport.

Feuz converted Piz Gloria's interior to a public restaurant immediately after shooting completed. Photos show an open interior

LEFT: Piz Gloria, Schilthorn Peak, Switzerland, ca. 1970 **BELOW**: Piz Gloria restaurant interior, ca. 1970

Revolving restaurant
on Mount Tsukuba,
Japan, 2005

space with the central stationary core accommodating a bar, some tables, a fireplace, and the stairway up from the lower level. The ring-type turntable surrounding this core had simple tables and chairs. When it opened in July 1969 the restaurant retained the name Piz Gloria. From the outset, Feuz and his team understood the promotional and theming possibilities presented by its association with the Bond franchise. Coasters, placemats, menus, brochures, and innumerable souvenirs in the gift shop referenced the restaurant's role in the film. The well-known 007 logo was stenciled on the waystation walls and clips from the film were shown in a small exhibit space below the heliport.

In the years following Schilthorn's construction and promotion around the world, three additional rotating restaurants were built in the Alps. In Argentina's Patagonia region, the country's only revolving restaurant caps the Andean summit of Cerro Otto. Other mountaintop revolving restaurants include one atop Mount Tsukuba in Japan and in Mussoorie, an Indian Hill Station in the Himalayan foothills.

Whether on a tower, shopping center, or mountain top, all revolving restaurants had glazed exterior walls. When canted to reduce reflections and present a fuller view to diners, they lent the structure a raked and speedy profile. Green, gold, and violet tinted glass were used occasionally to complement a particular exterior design. Window framing was most commonly of simple vertical mullions, but diamond lattice divisions have also been used. With few exceptions, the exterior glass walls of these restaurants were fixed; only the interior turntable rotated.

While revolving restaurant designs and the structures that hosted them could be separated into a number of formal categories, their interiors seemed to exhibit little variation. This was especially the case in the 1970s and later, when many revolving restaurants were operated by hotel chains. Novelist Geoff Nicholson, writing in the *New York Times* in the 1990s, described two designs that were unnerving in their similarities. He first dined at the Westin Harbour Castle Hotel in Toronto, Canada. "Then," Nicholson wrote, "I visited my second revolving restaurant, The View, at the Marriott Marquis in midtown Manhattan, for cocktails this time. And I was stunned. The dimensions, the layout, the look, the feel, were all exactly like the one in Toronto; I felt as if I were in an 'Outer Limits' episode."[21]

Consistency of interior layouts from one restaurant to the next is partly attributable to the nearly ubiquitous use of ring-type turntables. The circular plan and turntable rotating around a fixed service core ensure that patrons can enjoy views unobstructed by other parts of the building. Tables are usually arranged radially along the turntable so that all diners can face the glass. In ring-type revolving restaurants every seat has an equal claim on the view, no table is better than any other, and all take their turn adjacent the kitchen and bathroom entrances. The

stationary central core includes varying combinations of elevators, stairways, restrooms, and food prep and storage spaces. This arrangement keeps service areas out of the way and avoids the need for swiveling fixtures or connections. Where space is especially tight or building codes restrictive, kitchen facilities are placed on an adjacent floor level, on the ground floor, or menu items are limited to cold servings.

The standard package of fully glazed exterior walls, a circular plan with fixed and moving sections, and limited space in the central core, presented a creative challenge to interior designers. Often there was also a conscious intention not to compete with the view beyond the glass walls. Overly ostentatious or colorful interiors with eye-catching patterns were thought to detract from the restaurants' main feature and could potentially be reflected on the glass. Some designs had low-backed booths, others had tables that were not fixed in place. When space permitted, an inner and an outer ring of tables were used (with the inner ring typically raised a step or two above the outer ring), in part to break up what could otherwise be a monotonously uninterrupted and undifferentiated interior.

Although the ring turntable was most common, some restaurants followed the Australian Skyway model, featuring a disk-shaped turntable that was fully exposed with no stationary center—like a lazy Susan rather than a carousel. The kitchen, restrooms, and other service spaces were located off to the side, and therefore could be conventional in design. These disk turntables were often used when the restaurant was set within the

Top of the Tower restaurant in the Post Office Tower featured a subdued interior meant to not detract from the view outside, 1967

building form and the view was less than 360 degrees.[22] While disk turntable interiors were more spacious and allowed views across the entire room, there were tradeoffs. Tables in the center seemed to move at a different rate than those on the perimeter and thus could be disorienting. Their views were also obstructed by diners along the edge. Most importantly, dining rooms that revolved in their entirety drew the visitors' attention inward and distracted from the view.

Mechanically, both types of turntables relied on fairly simple technology: they were powered by a low-output electric motor, and the roller apparatus was often no more complicated than rubber wheels riding a steel track. Turntables were occasionally built by local contractors, but as the trend boomed in the 1960s, one company took a leading role in their design and manufacture. Based in Connecticut, Macton Corporation began in 1947 with a revolving stage design for the Jones Beach Marina on Long Island. Their steel turntables were eventually used in

almost 100 revolving restaurants built in the United States and abroad. In recent years, as revolving restaurant construction has shifted to the East, Chinese companies, such as the Shenyang-based Weizhong, have grown to serve that market.

Whether custom designed or from a major manufacturer, all restaurant turntables had to provide motion without the physical sensation of movement. Rattling tableware, squeaky machinery underfoot, even ripples in the water glasses were unacceptable. Companies developed informal methods to assess the quality of their work. Installations were considered successful if the ash remained on a cigarette standing upright on a plate or if a penny stayed set on its edge on the table through several rotations.[23]

Revolving restaurants were often accompanied by other levels with additional attractions. Stationary observation decks, bars, cafes, gift shops, and exhibition space provided a faster, more affordable opportunity to experience the view. In some structures these decks were connected by a stairway curving within the stationary core, and the observation deck doubled as a waiting area for the dining room. In others, the restaurant and the observation deck appealed to different clientele, a distinction illustrated in John Updike's 1986 novel, *Roger's Version*. The book's middle-aged main character begins his visit to a revolving restaurant in the underground parking garage:

> The elevator swooped to a stop to collect other passengers on the ground floor—tourists clutching guidebooks and cameras and wearing running shoes, heading for

the viewing platform; businessmen already clothed in summer suits of gray and putty heading for an expense-account lunch… then out we stepped, the tourists one way to the *Sky View* and its souvenir shops and constantly replaying tape of the city's history as intoned by some funeral director, and we onto the hushing steel-blue carpeting of *Restaurant 360*, its velvet ropes, its jungle ferns, its muffled tinkle of cutlery, its floor-to-ceiling windows overlooking the blocks and parks sixty stories below.[24]

Futuristic Designs and Theming

A visit to a revolving restaurant was not supposed to be just another night out. Of course, the primary experience was to eat while on a rotating floor high above the ground. Many restaurants furthered this experiential offering with little more than a name—La Ronde, 360, The View, The Carousel—a logo, and cleverly named dishes. Others presented a more immersive experience with the entrance, elevators, interior design, furnishings, and wait staff uniforms all working together, carrying connotations that cumulatively expressed a unified theme.

Like Disneyland's Main Street or twenty-first-century fast-food outlets modeled after 1950s diners, revolving restaurants reflect the power of narrative, the human desire to be told a story, to be a part of that story, and to feel a connection with a particular place and time. They offer the opportunity to escape daily life. In their influential study of the Las Vegas Strip, architects Robert Venturi, Denise Scott Brown, and Steve Izenour note that "essential to the imagery of pleasure-zone architecture are lightness, the

quality of being an oasis in a hostile context, heightened symbolism, and the ability to engulf the visitor in a new role: vacation from everyday reality."[25]

Most commonly the theme in revolving restaurants was a blend of high technology, futurism, and space travel. In the West and the Eastern Bloc, the postwar era was also the space age, when car designs, television programs, and gas station canopies reflected popular interest in space flight, rockets, and utopian visions of interplanetary exploration. From the Space Needle on, revolving restaurant designers embraced these trends—promotional literature described the Needle's original paint scheme as "Galaxy Gold," "Orbital Olive," and "Re-entry Red." Towers looked like rockets poised for liftoff; disk-shaped heads resembled flying saucers. While the world waited for rocket packs, underwater resorts, and moon colonies, diners could experience the future today on board a revolving restaurant. The attractions brought a bit of NASA to middle America; a bit of Vostok to Alma-Ata.

In co-opting the cultural cache of space travel, designers sought to make visitors feel, if only for an hour, that they were part of an advanced age; that by passing through the high-tech entryway, they were leaving the present behind and stepping into a privileged tomorrow. The entrance galleries and the elevators that whisked diners upward distanced ordinary life on the ground from the otherworldliness of the circular restaurant above. Typical was the journey described in the souvenir booklet for the Post Office Tower in Britain, "the visitor steps into one of two high-speed lifts for a miniature journey into space. The lift carries him smoothly upward, through the very heart of the Tower, to a vast window on the whole of London."[26]

Dreams of life among the clouds in glass-walled towers were not new.[27] In the twentieth-century sky living was a common theme of futurists, fantasy and pulp science fiction writers, architects, utopian theorists, and moviemakers who promised a not-too-distant world of residences, offices, spaceports, and whole cities perched on the tops of slender pillars.[28] Implicit in many of these visions was a desire to start afresh, to abandon Earth's sullied surface for a hermetically sealed techno-topia in the sky. It was no coincidence that many American postwar revolving restaurants were part of modernist urban redevelopment schemes seeking to remake declining downtowns and promising an exciting future, or at least an up-to-date today. Ironically, such large-scale renewal projects often left in their wake highways and vast vacant lots with little visual appeal from above.

While revolving restaurants were ostensibly places to dine and drink, food was, especially in the early years, more of an accoutrement, a supporting role for the main act, the view. Both nature and the human built landscape were set off by the height of the restaurant and the ritual of arrival. The world was observed but distant behind thick glass that muffled its sirens and horns. Revolving restaurants provided a summary orientation for out-of-towners and a new perspective for locals.

The locations of various revolving restaurants, however, suggest that a stunning view was not required. As a *New York Times* review observed, "the inspiration for a rotating restaurant in downtown Stamford is certainly curious, considering that the view slowly rotisseried in front of one's eyes is of railroad tracks, warehouses, and the Connecticut Turnpike."[29] The fictitious revolving restaurant in John Updike's novel overlooked "decaying old commercial buildings of brick and tar and a battered expressway in the throes of being widened."[30] Then, the simple experience of dining while in motion was considered allure enough.

Rotating Restaurants as Status Symbols

Tied to futurism, progress, and technological savvy, it is no wonder that from their beginnings rotating restaurants were icons of achievement and status. Rotating restaurants (especially those perched atop 500-foot-high towers) were a reassuring sign that a country or city was up-to-date. A 1970s ad campaign for the State of Georgia used John Portman's hotel restaurant to confirm that the state was a modern and vital part of America. One of these advertisements asked, "Hillbillies? You won't find them dining in a revolving restaurant-lounge atop the breathtaking Atlanta Skyline."[31]

For emerging places around the world, like post-Colonial African nations, the so-called "Asian Tigers," and former Soviet republics in Central Asia, revolving restaurants were prestigious symbols of arrival. In Africa during the 1960s and '70s, states newly formed from disparate tribes, languages, and histories considered grand projects like towers with rotating restaurants, palaces, and even whole new resort cities and capitals a means of engendering a national identity. Some in Africa and in the developed world saw them as worthwhile initiatives around which the new citizenry could coalesce and overcome differences. Writing about such projects, including an uncompleted tower and rotating restaurant in Zaire, the *New York Times* noted that "the overriding political priority for most, if not all, African states is the task of national consolidation. They contend that in all such attempts to fuse a national identity, prestige has often been more important than programs."[32] From their slowly turning platforms visitors were to survey how the cities had expanded, bringing progress to the landscape below. Whether for private civic boosters and developers of North America or central planning committees of Eastern Bloc countries, rotating restaurants served all ideologies and could fit any narrative. One of the most symbolically weighted tower and revolving restaurant constructions was the Fernsehturm (Television Tower) constructed in East Berlin.

On October 3, 1969, East German President Walter Ulbricht, along with several other Communist Party dignitaries, sat down to dinner in the Telecafé, a revolving restaurant atop the newly completed Fernsehturm. After five years of planning and construction, their gathering marked the formal opening of the 1,200-foot-tall tower, and with it, what they considered a big step forward in their postwar competition with the West. The tower—its looming presence visible throughout the divided city—was a practical tool to broadcast television signals across Berlin as well as a political symbol of East Germany's arrival as a modern, technological force.[33]

The Fernsehturm's tapered concrete shaft extends upward from a two-story ground-level entrance pavilion that, with folded-plate concrete roofs, resembles wings or rocket fins. Doors, stair balusters, and other decorative features inside the pavilion carry circular and spherical motifs evocative of the tower head and rotating restaurant. The steel head is 650 feet above the ground, 105 feet in diameter, and encloses seven levels. Covered by stainless steel panels with pyramidal reliefs, its appearance was undoubtedly meant to recall Sputnik, the first artificial satellite launched by the Soviet Union in 1957.[34] Within, there is an enclosed, stationary observation deck and the Telecafé one floor above. Upper floors contain television and radio equipment and are not open to the public.

Walter Ulbricht (center) and other East German dignitaries at a dinner inaugurating the new Telecafé and Fernsehturm, 1969

A visit to the tower includes encounters with features and spaces that reinforced the structure's overarching techno-astronautical theme. The open ground-floor pavilion and aerodynamic ticket booths lead to a circular elevator lobby with canted walls and stylized light fixtures—subdued lighting and angled walls make the lobby seem like a subterranean chamber. By depriving visitors of sensory clues to orient themselves, the experience of first encountering the view at the top is intensified. The restaurant's ring-type turntable originally had fixed seating for two hundred diners at tables placed radially along the perimeter. A large faceted glass mosaic depicts the Milky Way on the partition stair wall, and as a final touch, the wait staff originally had uniforms modeled after those worn by stewardesses.

As their table made a circuit along the canted glass every half hour, Dr. Ulbricht and his guests took in a panorama of the divided city. Empty lots, cleared of ruins after the war, were plentiful. Also plainly visible was the scar of the Berlin Wall. Visitors to the Telecafé in the 1970s and early 1980s recall that the tables had maps that left blank the area beyond the wall.[35] But that opening night the diners surely focused their attention on the new construction that was remaking this central area of Berlin. Like many revolving restaurant–equipped structures in the United States, the Fernsehturm was a primary component of a larger urban redevelopment initiative. The tower was considered a suitable substitute for a high-rise government building that was planned but never realized. By meeting the technological challenges of building such a structure, leaders of the German

TOP LEFT: Illustration of Telecafé from innaugural brochure, 1969 BOTTOM LEFT: Wait staff uniforms for the Telecafé were modeled after those of stewardesses, 1969 RIGHT: The Fernsehturm was part of the large-scale postwar redevelopment of the area around Alexanderplatz, East Berlin.

Democratic Republic meant to show
that they could match, and even outdo, the
West. The tower and its restaurant evoked
high technology and space travel, central
battlegrounds of the Cold War. They projected economic and technological vigor
that the GDR wanted its rivals and its own
citizens to appreciate.

In more recent years, governments
continue to regard revolving restaurants as
an important feature of high-profile, high-
prestige construction projects. Undoubtedly
the most ambitious was the Ryugyong Hotel
in Pyongyang, North Korea, started in 1987.
The 105-story building, which resembles a
flattened and bent ziggurat, was to have
exterior walls of mirrored glass and 3,000
guest rooms. Several disk-shaped floors projecting beyond the rectilinear facade near the
building's peak were to house five separate
revolving restaurants. However, in 1992 the
project ran out of money. Since then the hulk-
ing concrete shell has remained empty, its
construction crane still hovering over the site.
For the time being foreign tourists, business-
people, and functionaries desiring to eat
dinner in motion above Pyongyang have to
settle for the revolving restaurant atop the
45-story Kyoro Hotel.[36]

The Ryugyong was one of more than a
hundred revolving restaurant projects Asian
governments undertook in the last thirty
years that shifted the center of revolving restaurant construction from West to East. Since
the North American and European market
for new revolving restaurant installations
slowed to a near standstill in the mid-1980s,
most new revolving restaurant construction
has occurred in the Middle East, the South

Pacific, and Asia. As China's rapid economic
growth and urbanization accelerated, revolving restaurants have become an iconic
attraction in its booming cities. Some,
like Shanghai and Beijing, have more than
one. These revolving restaurants and their
host structures were assertions of modernity,
progress, and parity with the West.

In 1986 entrepreneur Weizhong Xu
opened a revolving restaurant in the Chinese
port city of Qinhuangdao. Recognizing the

Unfinished
Ryugyong Hotel in
Pyongyang, North
Korea, 2007; upper
floors were to house
five revolving
restaurants.

TOP: Weizhong restaurant project with support wheels in place before steel turntable
RIGHT: After steel turntable frame and deck installation

Oriental Pearl Tower, Shanghai, China

Interior of the Oriental Pearl restaurant

growing popularity of revolving restaurants and the opportunity to improve upon existing turntable technology, Weizhong Xu developed a new pin-gear system to drive the rotating floor. He took out a Chinese patent in 1988 and created a corporation to manufacture the system three years later. Based in Shenyang, the Weizhong Revolving Machinery Company has manufactured and installed over one hundred revolving restaurants in fifteen TV towers and eighty-five high-rise buildings during its first decade of operations.[37] Most were in Asia, but the company has also supplied machinery for restaurants in Albania, Kosovo, Saudi Arabia, Egypt, and Uganda. Weizhong's most notable installation was in what is probably the best known revolving restaurant in Asia, the one atop the Shanghai Oriental Pearl Tower.

Completed in 1995, the Oriental Pearl Tower stands over 1,500 feet tall. It is the largest tower in Asia and the third tallest tower in the world. Three cylindrical shafts form a central column that stretches between large lower and upper spheres, and the column is supported by three legs that spread outward from the lower sphere to the ground. The legs sweeping upward, combined with the graduated nature of the construction, narrowing from bottom to peak, suggest an over-inflated Eiffel Tower in rounded concrete, while the spheres seem to reference Berlin's Fernsehturm.

Though referred to as a television tower, the Oriental Pearl is also an entertainment and shopping center; its spheres contain several cafes and bars, a disco, conference hall, exhibition space, shops, an observation deck, and the revolving restaurant in the upper sphere. Like the Kuwait Towers, the Reunion Tower in Dallas, and the Milad Tower in Tehran, the restaurant's windows are framed with a diagonal latticework that is carried prominently across the entire surface of the head's exterior. The Pearl's interior is more spacious than most revolving restaurants, both in floor area and the height of the windows and ceiling.

Fading Appeal

From their earliest years, revolving restaurants received a mixed reception from architectural and travel writers, urban planners, conservationists, food critics, and the general public. For all the newspaper articles excitedly announcing plans for new revolving restaurants, there seems to be an equal number that labeled them gimmicks and a "tiresome touch."[38] Their widespread popularity in the West during the 1960s and '70s may have contributed to this ambivalence, as the concept evolved from curiosity to cliché. Owners found that rotation alone was no longer sufficient to attract customers and make repeat patrons of the locals. As the novelty of revolving restaurants wore off in North America and Europe during the 1980s and '90s, disenchantment seemed to grow.[39] Critics often pronounced the food an afterthought. Prices were high, and lingering over the view was discouraged. In essence, revolving restaurants were tourist traps.

Some thought the view was best from the revolving restaurant not because of its great height, but because the view did not include the restaurant itself.[40] From the ground, the towers were impossible to ignore and thus criticized for despoiling the settings they were

"I'm not that hungry!"

A 1962 cartoon by Alan Dunn published in the *New Yorker*, suggesting that the public was not universally enamored of the concept of a revolving restaurant. © The New Yorker Collection, 1962, Alan Dunn from cartoonbank. com. All Rights Reserved.

meant to showcase. A comment often heard in developing countries was that revolving restaurants were wasteful extravagances that served only the wealthiest citizens, foreigners, and business people.[41]

After the revolving restaurant's heyday in the United States and Europe, they were considered by some to be premier examples of kitsch. Outdated and out of style, their slow rotation was ho-hum in a hyper age. They were visited with irony, and with tongue in cheek. As a 1997 *Fortune* magazine article stated, revolving restaurants were "fun for holidays, like…April Fool's Day."[42] These attitudes were reflected in popular films and television programs that used revolving restaurants as the setting for absurd spectacles. The climactic scene in the popular Indian film *Naseeb* (1981) featured an elaborate brawl in a revolving restaurant that included members of rival gangs dressed as matadors, the Marx Brothers, and Charlie Chaplin. The open turntable spins out of control, setting fire to the interior and requiring an escape by zip line. Purchased with ill-gotten gains and representative of the antagonists' self-indulgent highlife, the restaurant is totally destroyed.

A year later, the Canadian television comedy series SCTV aired an episode that satirized the 1974 thriller *The Towering Inferno*, in which trapped victims must escape from a burning skyscraper.[43] The SCTV version, exaggerating the disaster-film genre to humorous excess, tells the story of opening night for a 280-story office building proudly labeled the highest, thinnest, and cheapest in the world. The fictional building was topped with a head structure that included a nuclear reactor and Johnny Nucleo's Top of the Reactor revolving restaurant. A local TV news reporter described the structure as "the classic paradox of the sublime and the ridiculous." A conflagration later in the evening followed by a mishap with the fire department results in the restaurant being launched on a suborbital trajectory into the Pacific Ocean. Both the film and TV program present the revolving restaurant as an example of technology run amok. In these narratives, revolving restaurant builders and those who buy into the concept reach too high, pay the price, and fall back to earth.

During the revolving restaurant's first decades it was often considered a symbol of urban pride and harbinger of a dynamic future. Along with the towers and structures they crowned, revolving restaurants were a vote of confidence in American cities at a time of depopulation and disinvestment. In Europe they accompanied needle-shaped television transmission towers as representations of postwar recovery and technological advancement. For emerging cities and nations around the world they continue to function as status structures.

The postwar era saw the construction of more revolving commercial buildings than any time in the past. The number of rotating theater stages and auditoria built during this period also exceeded those realized in the past. Revolving designs offered new ways of experiencing the world. Restaurants could distill a tourist's itinerary down to just an hour of bird's-eye observation. Postwar rotating theater stages furthered advances developed earlier in the century, while revolving auditoria liberated playwrights, designers, performers, and audiences from the traditional proscenium. As these projects moved forward designers of revolving residences continued to explore new forms and configurations that would satisfy individual aspirations, appeal to potential customers, and make the turning house and high rise a common and unexceptional building form.

CHAPTER FOUR

THE POSTWAR REVOLVING RESIDENCE

As Americans in the 1940s began to consider life in a postwar era, many architects and inventors searched for new house forms that would be appropriate to the upcoming age. They developed means of prefabrication to help meet the huge demand for housing. Visionary designers like Buckminster Fuller worked with new materials, structural shapes, and mechanized features and furnishings, anticipating a new future of high-tech homes that could be mass produced, easily transported, and in some cases rotated. Magazine articles, books, and films both during and in the years after the war anticipated the construction of new types of homes that would have little in common with traditional forms. In 1944, the *Chicago Daily Tribune* echoed these predictions, noting that "revolving houses are one of the post-war innovations to which we may look forward."[1]

Some assumed that these new houses would be embraced and promoted by all segments of American society. In Donald Hough's 1946 comedic novel *The Camelephamoose*, about returning soldiers adjusting to a postwar commercial culture, one character proclaims, "we're going into the greatest manufacturing and sales period the world has ever known"; "in the new houses—the new revolving houses, by the way, are already on the market—everything will be either of plastic or some other material."[2] Later, a character exasperated by the changes afoot and the seemingly contradictory conflation of terminology asks "what in the devil is a revolving house?"[3]

As manifestations of progress and portents of the future, rotating houses generated excitement. But cultural references also suggest that, as in the prewar period, this interest was accompanied by mixed feelings about how technology would affect established definitions of the home and hearth. The 1950 Red Skelton film *The Yellow Cab Man* featured a rotating house exhibited at a Los Angeles home show.[4] In a scene reminiscent of Keaton's haywire house in *One Week*, the model home malfunctions and, spinning out of control, throws visitors through the doors and windows.

Such endings to the hopes of rotating-house inventors were a common theme threaded through popular accounts of other once-new innovations introduced into the home, from toilets to televisions. Architecture scholar Mike Weinstock has written that the reaction to emerging home technologies, like those depicted in *The Yellow Cab Man*, is not new: "dystopian anxieties are strongly marked in literature and films, as if a measure of the anticipated effectiveness of any new technology is the peculiar mixture of dread and excitement it engenders; there is a narcotic dimension to society's dreams of interacting with technology."[5]

Mobility and Architecture

Despite this cultural trepidation, the postwar era saw a renewed emphasis on merging mobility and architecture. In the 1950s and '60s, Hungarian-born architect Yona Friedman developed designs for what he called "mobile architecture." His conceptual Spatial City was a shifting collection of stacked modules mounted on piles above an existing metropolis or otherwise unbuildable space; it was to be fully demountable and moveable. Like a rotating house, the Spatial City allowed occupants to easily transform their built environment and its orientation to the outside world. His designs were flexible, allowing inhabitants to modify them in response to shifting social and emotional needs. Friedman believed that buildings should belong to their occupants, that designers have too much control.

Ideas about movement in architecture were paralleled by new currents in painting and sculpture. Kinetic artists like Nicolas Schöffer sought new ways to represent movement and time in art. Schöffer's experimental kinetic towers explored a reciprocal relationship between the work of art and those in its surrounding environment, where structure and inhabitant responded to each other. Revolving architecture also reveals these added dimensions. The rotatable house could accommodate its occupants' way of living and changing conditions with just the push of a

button. Aware of their direct control over the structure's orientation and interior conditions, residents developed empowered views about their role vis-à-vis architecture and the environment.

As in the first half of the century, the postwar era saw the design of numerous proposed revolving residences. However, unlike the previous period, many in the 1960s and beyond were actually built. Their designers shared most of the same reasons that motivated work on turning buildings in the past—controlling exposure to daylight and other weather conditions and regulating the view.

While well-known architects are responsible for some of the projects conceived during this period, many were designed by professionals in other (often allied) fields who lacked formal architectural training. Builders, engineers, industrial designers, and independent inventors were all attracted to the challenge of creating distinctive structures that turned. Usually the house was for personal use, though the possibilities of profitable patents and mass production often arose later. Most rotating house designers seem to have come upon the idea on their own. Instances of influence or a progression of development from one project to the next are rare.

As in the prewar era, rotating houses generally assumed one of two forms: those that had internal turntables rotating a section of the house (often partitioned for various functions) and those in which the main section of the structure rotated in its entirety. Seeking convenience, efficiency, and novelty, designers developed new rotating and

Revolving kitchen exhibited at 1968 Ideal Home
Show in Olympia, England

pivoting features that updated earlier inventions. Tabletop lazy Susans enjoyed a popular resurgence.[6] Rotating cupboards that made better use of corner space in small kitchens became a popular option for new homes and remodeling projects.

The Daily Mail Ideal Home Exhibition, Britain's largest annual home fair, featured several of these innovations. In 1968 the show included a design in which the entire kitchen rotated. News coverage of the event stated, "gone are the days when kitchens were just unglamorous places in which to cook meals. This is the press button chromium-plated age of functional gimmickry. Here for instance the lady of the house doesn't have to move, the kitchen does it for her."[7] Revolving kitchens and other postwar efforts to increase efficiency bear some resemblance to the designs of Catharine Beecher and other reformers from the past. But for Beecher, efficient tools and systems glorified the role of women as scientific managers and household engineers; in the 1950s and '60s modern conveniences like electric can openers and rotating kitchens were promoted as means of escaping demeaning household work for more leisure time with the family.

Rotating features were marketed by home furnishing companies, appliance manufacturers, builders selling spec homes in suburbia, and lifestyle magazines. In 1964 *Playboy* magazine published designs for the Playboy Town House, a four-story, tangerine shag and teak–finished high-tech bachelor pad that had as its crescendo a fully outfitted bed. First introduced in a 1959 issue, the Playboy Bed rotated so that the occupant(s) could look out upon city views and then,

The Skarbergs' retracting bar, ca. 1955

"if we wish we can turn the bed so that we face the gemütlich warmth of the uni-bilt fireplace set against the stone wall."[8] The attached headboard included a built-in bar and refrigerator, as well as a telephone and push-button control panel for the lighting, window shades, and hi-fi.

Playboy's short-lived television program *Playboy's Penthouse* was filmed on a set made to resemble another bachelor pad, this one featuring a rotating bookcase that turned into a bar. The bookcase-bar was fitting furniture for the type of postwar bachelor the magazine was trying to attract and mold: erudite yet social, sophisticated, a bit whimsical, and gadget-savvy.[9] Creative homeowners also developed rotating devices to personalize their space and make it more flexible and adaptable to individual needs and desires. For example, Esther Skarberg and her husband wanted a bar in their California living room available for entertaining, but not during the rest of the day, so they developed a ring-shaped bar top that rotated into the wall and out of the way when cocktail time was over.[10]

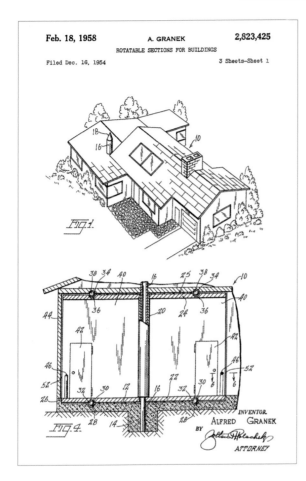

Alfred Granek's patent for an internally rotating house, 1954

and bedroom set; spacing of the partitions could be varied to suit the owner's wishes.[11] Because the ranch house was more spacious than a prewar urban apartment, Granek's design did not make use of the retractable furnishings that were the focus of Cimini's and Tate's patents from the early 1900s. Larger turntable sections, conventional furniture, and access to doors on the turntable enabled occupation of those partitioned spaces that were not facing the main living area. The design, therefore, was significantly more practical than those in which only one section of the turntable could be used at a time. A lack of retractable gagetry and the use of hand power to rotate the turntable suggests that the inventor was earnest about developing a new house type that would be taken seriously.

At rest, the only indication there was anything unusual about Granek's house was the turntable's central shaft extending through the roof (which was an unnecessary affectation). Otherwise it was similar to the millions of other houses built in suburban developments throughout the period. Granek figured that only by adopting an outwardly conventional form would his house have any hope of broad acceptance from potential homeowners and the banks and home-financing agencies that considered unusual designs risky investments. Yet despite his efforts there is no known record that Granek's house was ever constructed. The concept of an internally rotating house would not be picked up again until fifty years later in Germany, by a designer who had no interest in blending in.

Postwar Internally Rotating Houses

Prewar plans for internally rotating designs focused on making city apartments more adaptable and spacious at a time of rapid urbanization. In the 1950s at least one internally rotating house design was meant to accompany mass suburbanization. Alfred Granek's 1954 ranch house proposal featured a sizable four-section turntable with plenty of room for a conventional dining table, sofa,

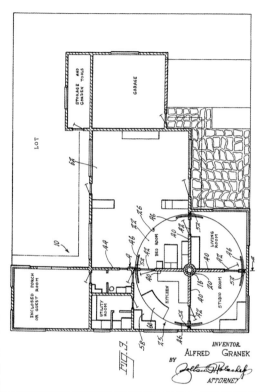

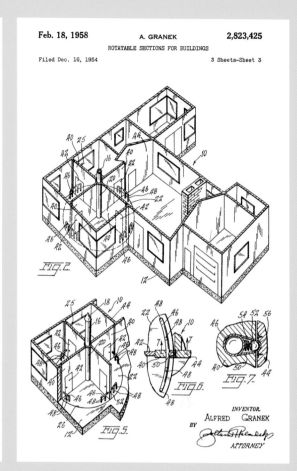

Alfred Granek's patent for an internally rotating
house, 1954

Rotor Haus

The German firm Hanse Haus is one of the largest prefabricators in Europe. It offers a variety of customizable permanent house designs, retirement homes, and vacation houses featuring patented wall systems and eco-friendly materials and technologies. In 2004, the company was looking for a way to celebrate its seventy-fifth anniversary, generate some publicity, and counter public perceptions that prefabricated house designs had to be rectilinear and unoriginal.[12]

Hanse Haus contacted the German industrial designer Luigi Colani to propose a joint project, perhaps for a new attention-getting stairway model or other prefab component. Colani was a natural choice for a collaborator, well-known throughout Europe and Asia for his unorthodox industrial and consumer designs. His cars, trucks, planes, camera bodies, furniture, neckties, paintbrushes, doorknobs, infant bathtubs,

and urban plans have been featured in countless exhibitions, publications, and product lines. Often labeled futuristic, his work is inspired by the sleek profiles and curving lines of bird wings, shark bodies, and other natural forms. When Hanse Haus contacted him, he was also celebrating an anniversary, entering into his fiftieth year of design practice. Colani accepted their offer on the condition that he be allowed to adapt a project he had first worked on twenty years previous—the Rotor Haus.[13]

In the early 1980s, Colani developed a plan for a high-density urban development he called BioCity. Assuming the shape of a supine human body, its concentrated center resembled the head and torso, with more narrow residential districts extending outward across the landscape like arms and legs.[14] Each of the BioCity's limbs was to feature a pair of opposing terraces extending up the banks of a central waterway and populated with over 15,000 individual homes. Intended for construction near Asia's megacities, the individual BioCity houses were designed to derive the maximum amount of useable space from an extremely small footprint.[15] The interior consisted of a primary room with a turntable divided into three sections, each with furnishings and appliances corresponding to a different room function. The bath section featured a tub, sink, cabinet, and mirror; the kitchen section included an oven and stove, sink, countertops, and small pantry; and the bedroom section had a bed with storage beneath.

The Rotor Haus functioned much like the interior turntable designs from earlier in the century, of which Colani has said he was

Rotor Haus plan, 2004

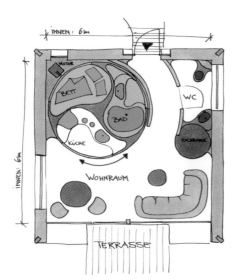

Rotor Haus prototype by Luigi Colani and Hanse
Haus, 2004. All Rotor Haus images courtesy
Hanse Haus, www.hanse-haus.com

Rotor Haus prototype interior, bath section

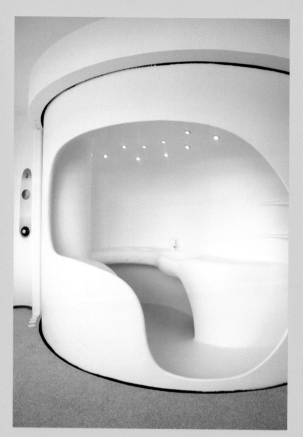 

LEFT: Rotor Haus prototype interior, kitchen section RIGHT: Luigi Colani in the Rotor Haus prototype, 2004

Rotor Haus prototype with the turntable's bed
section facing main living area

unaware.[16] Only one of the turntable's three sections was accessible at a time. The section in use opened onto the primary room with its large glass wall and a narrow partitioned toilet and storage space in the back corner. With the turntable rotated to open a particular section to the primary room, that space was effortlessly adapted to a variety of uses depending on the time of day and the needs of the occupant. "Why lose valuable space through halls and corridors when all the rooms you need can be built back-to-back and attainable at the touch of a button?" the designer asked.[17]

In the prototype Rotor Haus, a small electric motor connects to the turntable's central shaft via a motorcycle chain. A program regulates the turntable's speed, ensures that the turntable starts and stops smoothly, and turns the precise 120-degree rotation necessary to line up the desired interior section with the opening in the turntable partition. Occupants operate the electronics via a control panel on the adjacent wall.

Colani designed and fabricated the prototype's sectional turntable and the toilet/closet partition in his Karlsruhe workshop. Hanse Haus architect Annette Müller designed the exterior shell, which was built in the company's factory near the village of Obersleichtersbach. Her original designs were for a rectilinear box that would allow multiple Rotor Haus units to be stacked or arranged to provide expanded and varied forms. True to his voluptuous style, Colani sent her early sketches back with all the edges rounded and the exterior walls given a convex shape—as if the original design had been worked over on a belt sander.

The prototype's kitchen sink, stove, bath, and toilet are fiberglass and non-functional (production models were to be of vacuum-injected plastic). In fact, sculpted without knobs, handles, or drains, they are more suggestive than literal. In the eggshell aesthetic of the finished turntable sections, as well as the oval door and window openings, there are similarities to works by architect, theater designer, and artist Friedrich Kiesler, especially his Endless House. This molded concrete design with no right angles was an exercise in synthesizing sculpture and architecture, first conceived in the 1930s and reworked over the next several decades. It received renewed attention in the 1960s as popular culture embraced plastic forms that anticipated planetary and lunar settlement.[18]

The partnership between Colani and Hanse Haus never went beyond the construction and promotion of the single prototype, despite significant popular interest in the concept. During its two-day grand opening over 3,000 people toured the house at Hanse Haus's headquarters. Magazine and newspaper articles in Germany and abroad featured the house, and it was highlighted on German TV and used as a backdrop in photo shoots for a variety of products and causes. All of this advertising, in which the prototype was referred to as the Hanse Colani Rotor House, provided a wealth of free publicity for both partners. Hanse Haus made valuable contacts with other architects, and potential customers lured to the headquarters to see the Rotor Haus discovered the more conventional models that were available for sale.[19]

Afterward Colani seems to have a mixed opinion of the project. In discussing the history of the design, he calls the turntable a gimmick and talks about how "we were laughing all the time when we were building this stupid thing."[20] Alternately, he asserts his ownership of the concept and hopes to eventually find a firm that is willing to mass-produce them.

Externally Rotating Houses

Some of the first externally revolving houses constructed in the postwar era appear to have been modest vacation homes meant for part-time living. That some designers chose to experiment with rotating structures as leisure-time getaways is not surprising. The 1950s and '60s saw a boom in vacation home construction in the United States and Western Europe. Postwar second homes meant only for occasional use offered designers the chance to try out creative glazing and roof designs and whimsical structural forms.[21] Such designs offered a welcome break from the postwar landscape, increasingly dominated by standardized glass-box office buildings and suburban ranch houses. Through their second-home designs owners could unwind and assume their "true" persona: outdoor athlete, swinging single, family man.

Rotating Vacation Homes

Outside the California desert oasis of Palm Springs, down a sand-swept mile-long road, sits a small residential enclave called Snow Creek. Originally a failed olive farm, by the 1960s it included just a couple dozen houses sharing amazing views of the surrounding San Jacinto mountains. The area is known as a place for those who want to be left alone. In

1961 Los Angeles businessman Floyd D'Angelo purchased two acres in Snow Creek and constructed a revolving house to serve as a weekend retreat and setting to display his collection of African game trophies. D'Angelo decided to build the unusual structure in response to Snow Creek's particularly harsh climate and dramatic landscape. By remaining in motion throughout the day, the interior can be sheltered from direct sunlight (the region has an average of 350 sunny days per year) while still permitting unobstructed views of the surrounding mountains. It is unmistakably high-tech and futuristic.

D'Angelo owned the Aluminum Skylight and Specialty Corporation. Reflecting his appreciation for and ready access to the material he made extensive use of aluminum in his house. The polygonal exterior features alternating glass and solid canted triangular wall panels framed in aluminum. On the inside, aluminum open-web trusses supporting the roof radiate from the center to the exterior walls. The 750-square-foot interior is largely open, with a kitchen on one side of the door and aluminum partitions separating a bathroom and small study from the rest of the living space. Throughout, the walls, floor, carpet, partitions, cabinets, and refrigerator are mint green.[22]

Though D'Angelo was clearly an accomplished designer, he turned to his aerospace engineer friend Harry Conrey for help with the rotating components. All the mechanical equipment is beneath the raised house concealed behind a cement-block skirt wall. Steel struts with sixteen rubber tire casters extend downward from the underside of the house; the casters ride on an annular rail that sits on a

D'Angelo House, 2007

TOP: Kitchen, D'Angelo House, 2007
RIGHT: Underside of D'Angelo House showing
rotating track, toothed rack that engages
the electric-motor-powered pinion, and cement
block skirt wall, 2007

concrete-slab foundation. To rotate, a small electric motor drives a pinion that engages the toothed circular rack attached to the house frame. Plumbing runs inside the central column and connects through universal joints with stationary land pipes. A simple industrial cable that provides continuous electrical service wraps and unwraps around the central shaft.

Originally, a photovoltaic cell mounted on the roof synched to the electric motor that turned the house through its 130-degree arc. D'Angelo adapted the device from a product his company made to open and close aluminum louvers. At night a "time clock arrangement" returned the house to its original orientation or could be programmed to stop at a particular view. D'Angelo reported that it "revolves at such a slow rate of speed that there is no sensation of movement."[23]

One might assume that D'Angelo considered the house an experiment: the owner of an aluminum company exploring new markets for his products and testing the possibility of a prefabricated vacation home at a time when second homes were growing in popularity. But D'Angelo's nephew, who helped assemble the house when he was a teenager, claimed that his uncle had no such intention. The nephew, also named Floyd, said his uncle, "did not develop the house as a prototype for mass production. He was motivated for the fun of it. He was always involved in different projects like that."[24]

In 2002 Bill Butler of Palm Springs bought the house almost immediately after learning it was for sale. Because it hadn't been lived in for years, the house was in very poor shape: windows were broken, and the inside

Bill Butler on the D'Angelo House balcony, 2007

was filthy with grime and rotting carpet. The rotating motor was missing, and air-conditioning ducts added years before had been placed over the track, indicating that it was occupied for some time without the ability to turn. Structurally, though, the building was sound. Butler recalled, "The good news was that it had been neglected, and was, therefore, essentially unchanged from its original state."[25]

A fan of mid-century design, Butler was determined to return the house to its 1960s appearance and enable it to rotate again. He replaced all the deteriorated and missing mechanical systems, scrubbed the interior (using a toothbrush to clean the open-web ceiling trusses), repainted, and got the vintage

FIVE-FOOT-WIDE *deck surrounds cabin, nearly flush with adjoining concrete slab that helps extend outdoor living area. Cabin rotates so slowly that even small children can ride on and off the deck.*

It turns like a giant lazy Susan

ARCHITECT: HAROLD BARTRAM

Flip a switch and this cabin on Blakely Island, Washington, turns like a giant lazy Susan to catch the sun or view. It rides on eight plastic-faced wheels that run on a steel track bolted to a circular track. Two of the wheels are powered by a ¾-horse reversible gear motor controlled through low-voltage switching.

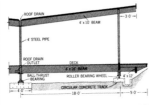

CABIN *turns 270° on central steel column on ball-thrust bearing. Flexible sections in water, sewer lines.*

THE OWNERS *fly here in 1½ hours from Kent, Oregon.*

CABIN *is then rotated so living room faces the sun.*

TOP LEFT: Harold Bartram's rotating vacation home on Blakely Island in *Sunset* magazine's book *Cabins and Vacation Houses*, ca. 1967
TOP RIGHT: Bruno Ghirelli's Rotating House in Noceto, Italy, ca. 1964 **RIGHT**: Bruno Ghirelli being interviewed for a news program, ca. 1964

kitchen working. After experimenting with various motor and gearing combinations, Butler and some colleagues also got the house to turn again. Today it starts a bit grudgingly with a faint grind and vibrates along at a noticeable pace.

At first glance Butler's house bears a definite resemblance to Max Taut's crystalline rotating house for the dunes at Königsberg. With multiple planes visible when stationary, both designs offer a heightened sense of movement and a constantly shifting perspective. The use of different exterior wall materials, however, reveals an important distinction between the two. Taut's glass walls celebrated transparency, light, and an openness to the environment. D'Angelo's Snow Creek house, with its solid panels and windows that seem to turn in upon themselves, is, in contrast, a protective cocoon, sheltering inhabitants from a hostile landscape and punitive sun.

A few years after D'Angelo finished his Snow Creek house, another amateur inventor set to work on his own concept for a rotating residence. Bruno Ghirelli owned a company that developed special-purpose construction and forestry vehicles in his hometown, Noceto, Italy. An interest in engines and racing led him to the world of go-carts, and in the late 1950s and early 1960s he established a team, participated in competitive go-cart races in public squares and on country roads, and built a permanent track in Fraore, near Parma. In 1964 he became best known for a "satellite villa" he built in Noceto.[26]

Ghirelli developed what he called the Casa Girevole (Rotating House) in collaboration with Swiss architect Ray Michellod and

patented the design the following year.[27] The two-bedroom steel-frame structure was supported awkwardly on a narrow steel column. Like the D'Angelo House, Ghirelli's design featured a photoelectric control that kept the house's movement synchronized with the sun. Pipes running through the central column supplied water tanks located above the ceiling, and a windmill located onsite provided some of the house's electrical supply. While Ghirelli's house had features that were high-tech for the time, it was (excepting its placement on the column) reserved and conventional in form and architectural detailing.

Back in the United States, George Wilson, an Oregon rancher and wheat farmer, decided to build a summer home on Blakely Island, one of the San Juan Islands, north of Seattle, Washington. The small community consisted at the time of both permanent homes and vacation homes. Because it was not connected to the mainland by bridge or regular ferry service, many residents were pilots who reached the island via private planes.[28]

An amateur aviator, Wilson asked local builder Harold Bartram to develop a home that could accommodate his desire to watch arrivals and departures on the adjacent runway. But Wilson's wife preferred to have the house oriented toward the water so that she could see boats pass by the windows. Bartram accommodated wife and husband with a hexagonal house set on a circular turntable flush with the ground.[29] Like many vacation homes from the period, it was clad in TI-II grooved plywood panels, featured large picture windows, and had an informal flow from interior to exterior. The turntable, which operated similar to Floyd D'Angelo's version, included a wood deck for outdoor living that continued the plank-like texture of the house's siding.[30] Bartram provided his clients a successful synthesis of contemporary tastes for second home design and the unique benefits of rotating construction.

Round and Polygonal Forms

The first examples of externally rotating homes meant for year-round use began to appear shortly after D'Angelo's house was completed. Like builder Sam Harkleroad's design constructed near Novato, California, in 1963, the majority featured cylindrical forms and round plans.[31] These designs (and, even more so, the growing number of round revolving restaurants) linked this building form in the public's consciousness with rotation to the point where many assumed all contemporary round and polygonal structures were meant to turn, from Bruce Goff's 1948 Ford House in Aurora, Illinois, to John Lautner's 1960 Malin Residence (the Chemosphere) in Los Angeles.[32]

Postwar rotating house designs were no doubt influenced by the Space Needle and other revolving restaurants that were concurrently spreading around the world. The many built revolving restaurants lent a degree of legitimacy to rotating design, showing that the idea was both technically feasible and not nausea-inducing. They also renewed interest in the use of rotation to capitalize on views and location. This outward-looking perspective explains in part the most common rotating house form that evolved during this period—round or polygonal in plan, glass walled, flat roofed, and often raised upon a narrow pedestal. With extensive glazing, clean lines, and a reliance on industrial materials, these homes trace their lineage to prewar modernist buildings. The cylindrical or polygonal form dates back even further.

According to nineteenth-century American phrenologist Orson Fowler, his designs for two-story octagonal homes made more efficient use of the exterior walls and allowed a greater amount of sunlight and ventilation to enter the residences than square houses. Fowler published the designs in his 1856 book, *A Home For All*.[33] High-tech for their time, the designs were to include central heating, indoor plumbing, and other modern conveniences. A few thousand octagonal houses based on Fowler's ideas were built through the turn of the century, primarily in New York, Massachusetts, and the Midwest.[34]

Perhaps the most obvious ancestor of the postwar rotating house form was the Dymaxion House, designed by R. Buckminster Fuller. First developed in the late 1920s, the Dymaxion (a conflation of "dynamic," "maximum," and "tension") was a hexagonal form set on a central column and secured by a series of cables zigzagging between the ground and the tip of the column. Above the enclosed living space was an open deck sheltered beneath a hipped roof.

The housing shortages of the post–World War II era and the potential to retool factories for peacetime production led Fuller to rework his design and renew efforts to get it manufactured. A cooperative venture with Beech Aircraft, the construction of a prototype home in Wichita, Kansas, and a flood of publicity prompted 37,000 unsolicited orders and

R. Buckminster
Fuller and his 1927
model of the
Dymaxion House

the serious interest of investors. However, Fuller soon realized the continuing challenges to mass-producing homes—from financing to resistance by the building trades—were insurmountable at the time. In the end, only two prototypes were ever constructed.

Though Fuller never intended the Dymaxion to rotate, the home was an explicit example of high technology infused with movement. It was inspired by the mass production and industrial processes of automobile manufacture, and its lightweight aluminum exterior looked like it belonged on an airplane. The 1927 version featured a spiraling worm gear elevator and a hangar below the raised floor to park an "amphibian airplane-automobile." The postwar version included "ovolving shelves" that tripled the capacity of a typical bureau by rotating vertically to recess stored items within the walls. Dymaxions were also to have pivoting closets that swung into the room to provide convenient access to the closet's contents. The industrial character of Fuller's design was further emphasized by its official name, the "Dymaxion Dwelling Machine."[35]

Five years after Fuller introduced the Dymaxion, architect George Fred Keck presented his own version of the futuristic model home. Its resemblance to postwar rotating

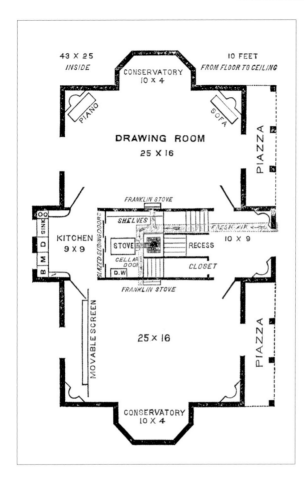

43 X 25
INSIDE

CONSERVATORY
10 X 4

10 FEET
FROM FLOOR TO CEILING

PIANO

SOFA

DRAWING ROOM
25 X 16

PIAZZA

FRANKLIN STOVE

SHELVES

FRESH AIR

GLAZED SLIDING DOORS

KITCHEN
9 X 9

STOVE

10 X 9

RECESS

CELLAR
DOOR

CLOSET

D.W

B M D

SINK

FRANKLIN STOVE

MOVABLE SCREEN

25 X 16

PIAZZA

CONSERVATORY
10 X 4

Concentration of circulation, service spaces, and mechanicals in the central core of a house designed by Catharine Beecher and Harriet Beecher Stowe in their 1869 book *The American Woman's Home*

designs is clear. Built as an exhibition home for the 1933 Century of Progress Exposition in Chicago, it featured three floors with polygonal plans. The lowest level accommodated an open porch, recreation room, and mechanical spaces; the floor above was the main living area; and the top floor had an open conservatory. Walls on the upper two levels were glazed from floor to ceiling. With its blinds drawn or curtains closed it looked like a giant steel-framed wedding

cake. Keck called his design the House of Tomorrow. As with the Dymaxion House, its ground-floor hangar anticipated a future in which homeowners would commute by aircraft.

Both the Dymaxion House and the House of Tomorrow had round central halls that accommodated a circular stairway as well as a core shaft serving as a channel for all the ducts, wires, and pipes coming into the houses. While such an arrangement was logical considering the buildings' circular form, it also reflected a desire to rationalize the organization of the complicated plumbing, HVAC, and electrical networks, long a concern of designers looking to make houses more efficient and easy to maintain and upgrade.[36] This approach was almost universally adopted by postwar revolving house designers, who found it well suited to the challenges of linking stationary and rotating parts of the building.

Postwar Futuristic Design

During the 1950s and '60s, satellites, transistors and integrated circuitry, automation and robotics, and manned space missions including the Apollo lunar landing program filtered down to popular culture, graphic and product design, fashion, and automotive and architectural design. The cultural fascination with space exploration and high technology that infused this era can be seen in the styling of postwar rotating houses. Circular rotating homes resembled the wheel-shaped space stations envisioned by scientists, writers, and filmmakers since the beginning of the century. Early conceptual space station designs were often cylindrical or toroidal

(doughnut-shaped) structures intended to rotate slowly on their axes to simulate gravity. In 1952 *Collier's* magazine published rocket engineer Wernher von Braun's ideas for manned space travel in a series of highly influential articles illustrated by Chesley Bonestell, a leading Hollywood matte painter who was originally trained as an architect. Bonestell's detailed paintings dramatically showed von Braun's toroidal three-level, eighty person space station rotating slowly in orbit above Central America.[37]

Similar designs for rotating space stations were featured in articles in *Boy's Life* and *Popular Mechanics* and in science-fiction and comic books such as *Mystery in Space*. They also appeared in films; in 1958 the Soviet movie *Road to the Stars* with its doughnut-shaped space station was released to audiences in the Eastern Bloc. Perhaps the most famous rotating space station was that seen in Stanley

Kubrick's 1968 film *2001: A Space Odyssey*. The double-decker Space Station V rotating to Richard Strauss's Blue Danube waltz remains one of the most iconic images of cinema history. All of these designs made the wheel and torus-shaped space station a well-known popular symbol for progress. Its form was adapted and referenced for a range of high-tech designs, most notably for tower head structures and postwar rotating houses.[38]

Another cultural product that both reflected and shaped popular perceptions of life in the future was the animated television situation comedy *The Jetsons*, first broadcast in September 1962.[39] Featuring the daily life of George Jetson, his wife Jane, and their children Judy and Elroy, the series presented a futuristic vision of life sometime in the twenty-first century. Prominent throughout every episode are labor-saving devices and high-tech tools that the show's creators, with

Chesley Bonestell's painting of Wernher von Braun's 1950s design for an Earth-orbiting space station

considerable satire, predicted were on the immediate horizon. Machines or robots do the real work, and everything is achieved at the push of a button, automatic and instantaneous. Machines, whether it was the "foodarackasackle" or a "digital index operator" were shown as both miraculous and mischievous, going berserk more often than working as intended.

The Jetsons lived in the Sky Pod Apartments. Their building, along with most others in the show, was round and had fully glazed exterior walls. They were perched on one or two slender shafts, so that the Jetsons' entire existence occurs above ground. Though none of the buildings seemed to rotate, similarities between the architecture depicted every week on *The Jetsons* and the towers and saucer-shaped, glass-walled revolving restaurants and revolving house designs that appeared in the 1960s is hard to miss.

The cartoon promised a future where everything was different and familiar at the same time. New technology offered the promise of a toil-free existence, yet continually failed to meet those expectations. Machines broke down, gadgets went haywire or created more work than there would have been were they not involved. Though framed in humorous situations, a distinctly dystopic thread runs through this vision of tomorrow. Projected into the future these concerns also reflected contemporary anxieties about an increasingly automated present. Like the depictions of revolving architecture in popular articles and films, *The Jetsons* reveals a culture-wide ambivalence over the effects of progress and the growing dependence on technology.

The Value of the View—Foster House

In 1967 architect Richard T. Foster set out to design his own residence for a secluded four-acre site in Wilton, Connecticut. After four attempts at a home that would adequately accommodate views of a nearby pond, reservoir, and woods, Foster gave up on a conventional approach. Eventually he developed a circular structure of reinforced concrete and steel with glazed exterior walls. To ensure that any room could enjoy any view at any time, he decided to make the house rotate.

Foster was first a student, then a protégé of Philip Johnson. He was architectural coordinator for the Seagram Building in New York City and had been involved in the design of several buildings for New York University, as well as the Kreeger Museum in Washington and the New York State Pavilion for the 1964 World's Fair (meant to represent the "County Fair of the Future"). The pavilion design included narrow observation towers that—with external elevators and disk-shaped heads—were similar to the TV towers sprouting across Europe. These structural forms were likely on Foster's mind as he worked through the design for his own residence.

The house in Wilton is raised on a stationary pedestal that includes a concrete core carrying plumbing, utility lines, and a spiral staircase linking the rotating section above with a ground-floor entrance. The glass-walled rotating superstructure has a series of wedge-shaped rooms extending out from a central foyer where the rotating section meets the fixed core and stairway. Foster adapted a three-ton ball-bearing assembly originally

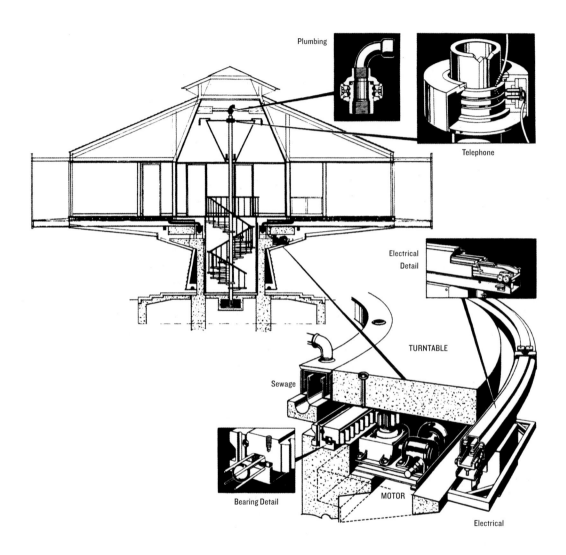

Plumbing

Telephone

Electrical
Detail

TURNTABLE

Sewage

Bearing Detail

MOTOR

Electrical

Foster House turntable and connections that
allow the house to rotate 360 degrees

designed for construction cranes and gun turrets and powered by a small electric motor to support and serve his house's rotating section. Using gaskets and troughs, feed-rail connectors, and swiveling ball joints, the assembly enables the house to turn a full 360 degrees while providing all the amenities of a conventional home.[40]

Like the Villa Girasole, the Foster House is a curious blend of contemporary and traditional design. Its UFO-like exterior form and materials, such as Cor-Ten steel and large sheet glass, suggest avant-garde modernism, while the wood shingled exterior cladding borrows from New England vernacular architecture. High-tech curves were molded with material historically used for fishing cottages. The weathered steel balcony with its patina of rust was both up-to-date (Picasso had just finished his Cor-Ten sculpture for Chicago's Daley Plaza) and organic in its emphasis on natural processes. Where the Girasole distinguished its traditional design elements from its modern features, dividing the structure in half, Foster synthesized old and new, creating an exceptionally well-balanced and entirely innovative composition.

In deciding to rotate the house Foster had little interest in that overriding motive shared by so many previous revolving designs: controlling sunlight and other weather conditions. Interviewed while the house was still under construction he said, "I didn't plan the house so that we could go riding. It was planned so that we could take advantage of the varied and beautiful views. We didn't try to capture the sun. There didn't seem to be any point in it."[41] Instead, Foster's goal was more closely aligned with

William Kent's, the designer of the eighteenth-century rotating shelter in Kensington Gardens. Both buildings focused attention on a vista unfolding below and into the distance. They turned in order to change—at the occupant's whim—a specific viewpoint.

The primacy of the view was not reflected only in extensive glazing and the ability to rotate. In the Foster House, and many other postwar rotating designs, the living area is raised up above ground level to maximize the view. This emphasis reflects the value (aesthetic and financial) placed on scenic vistas during this period, as the outside became an important component of the interior décor. As Foster recalled on the twenty-fifth anniversary of the house's construction, "someone said once, that it is a most expensive way to change the wallpaper, and they may be right."[42] But the Fosters, able to watch changing seasons, the annual arrival of migrating birds, and a day's sunrise and sunset from the same room or any room, found life in the house well worth the cost.

The Solar Structure—Rolf Disch's Heliotrop House

In the early 1990s German architect Rolf Disch designed his own residence for a hillside site near Freiburg, Germany. Disch had long been interested in green, energy-efficient design—in 1987 a solar car he developed won the Tour de Sol—so when he started on his own house, he was determined to make the most of energy-saving features and renewable resources. Called Heliotrop and completed in 1994, it was meant to showcase cutting-edge sustainable design and serve as a private residence and office for Disch and his

spouse. The three-story barrel-shaped house is set on a central pedestal and column that incorporates the rotating mechanism, pipes and ductwork, and a circular stairway. In some ways, it resembles Richard Foster's house topped with two additional levels. On the exterior, each floor has a pair of French doors opening onto metal catwalks supported by metal pipe frames extending from outriggers on the lowest floor level. The assembly suggests construction scaffolding yet to be removed, as if the house remains a work in progress. Corrugated metal panels cover parts of the facade that are not glazed. The interior contains a combination of living spaces (bedroom, kitchen, bath), offices, and meeting rooms. Disch introduced variety into each interior floor by staggering one or two step changes in the floor level.

While Disch used stock building materials on the exterior, he designed and fabricated the central column from scratch. Made of plywood panels over four inches thick assembled into a tube, the column (with some steel reinforcement) supports the entire construction. When Disch first started developing the all-wood design, no one knew how to bring it into being. After six months of experimentation and testing, Disch found an appropriate glue and plywood combination that was both sufficiently strong and flexible. The ball bearings and rotating mechanisms were also custom made.

Heliotrop utilizes solar energy in several ways. First, as its name implies, the house can be turned to track the sun. In cool seasons this allows whichever room the occupants prefer to remain in the sun's warming rays throughout the day. Alternately, like the Girasole and other rotating houses, the main living spaces can be shielded from direct midday sun by turning the entire structure so that those living spaces point north. This orientation, also like the Girasole, allows Heliotrop to face away from neighboring houses and into the hillside, lending its occupants a degree of privacy, seclusion, and enclosure.

During summer days the couple usually has the house facing north, up the hillside. In the evenings they rotate it to point the main living areas south. During colder months they rotate the house slowly, following the sun across the horizon. In addition to this hybrid passive system, an enormous rooftop photovoltaic array generates electricity. The solar panel can be turned independently of the rest of the house so that it faces the sun even when the inhabitants desire shade. Motors tilt the panel to maintain optimal exposure to sunlight or lay it flat for protection during storms. The panels and other systems make Heliotrop a positive-energy house; it feeds the excess electricity it generates into the power grid.

Heliotrop's green characteristics extend beyond rotating for light and shade and collecting solar rays for electrical power. The balcony railings on the lowest level have rows of clear pipes through which water flows and is gradually warmed by the radiant heat. Synchronizing the movement of the house with the sun's transit allows maximum exposure of this system to solar radiation. The house also has a geothermal pump system to help heat and cool the interior. Rainwater that falls onto the roof is collected in a cistern and filtered for use in the house.

OPPOSITE
Heliotrop House by
Rolf Disch, ca. 1994

TOP: Kitchen, dining room, and living room in Heliotrop House
RIGHT: The Heliotrop's central column
FAR RIGHT: Water is warmed by the sun as it circulates through clear pipes on the Heliotrop balcony railings.

Disch designed Heliotrop to be reproducible. He envisioned a time when the house could be prefabricated in a factory and easily shipped and assembled on site. Thus far he has built two other Heliotrop houses in addition to his own at Freiburg. In 1996 Disch's firm displayed a full-sized model at Swissbau, the international construction industry trade fair in Basel. This structure, identical to the Freiburg house, was preconstructed, then disassembled and shipped to Switzerland, reassembled for the show, then disassembled again and transported to Nuremberg. The firm built another Heliotrop as an exhibition building in Offenburg, Germany. There, the house served as a model setting for a bathroom fixture company. The Offenburg Heliotrop was identical to the others, except that it did not rotate.

As with the Villa Girasole, the Foster House, the Rotor Haus, and others, the Heliotrop was a source of curiosity among locals and those who read about it in the architectural press and other publications. "Every week we have people coming over who want to look and visit the house," Disch said.[43] The Heliotrop provides free publicity for his firm. It is an appealing three-story logo that highlights Disch's green design credentials and confirms that his ideas are not unbuildable fantasies.[44]

The Smart House—Johnstone House

When Al and Janet Johnstone married they decided to sell their existing homes and build a new one. They searched throughout the San Diego area looking for an ideal spot, until, in January 2001, Al came across a "for sale" sign on an overgrown lot on the side of Mount Helix in La Mesa. Returning with a machete, he discovered a small flat area and, recognizing the possibilities for a structure with amazing views, they promptly bought the land.

The Johnstones' new property presented a couple of interrelated challenges: how best to accommodate the panoramic views and how to make the most of the small buildable site. With vistas extending to the city below and eight mountains and the Pacific Ocean in the distance, they knew the orientation of rooms and windows would be central to the design's success. But they could only build on a small, flat portion of the site—constructing a conventional house across the steep hillside would have meant substantial additional costs and required a grading permit. The shape of the flat area suggested a circular form; Al Johnstone figured he could build a large round upper level atop a lower level with a smaller footprint matching the size of the pad. "And if you're going to have a round structure," he said, "why not make it rotate to have every view?"[45]

Johnstone may also have had in mind a couple buildings he had encountered years earlier. In the 1960s, he read a newspaper story about a proposed pair of twenty-five-story rotating towers for the beach in nearby La Jolla. In the following decade Johnstone came across a small 1950s-era rotating house in north central New Jersey. Years later he recalled that the 800-square-foot house was constructed atop a salvaged revolving gun turret and featured a rudimentary plumbing arrangement with a trough and flap that would certainly fail to meet current building codes.[46]

Al Johnstone fit well into the century-old tradition of individualist inventors who undertake rotating building projects. When he started designing the Mount Helix house he was a retired telephone company engineer and computer programmer who had previously served as his own contractor for a more conventional house. Throughout the design process his primary goal was to build a house that could rotate an unlimited number of times in either direction while providing all of the amenities (and more) of a stationary home and meeting all the necessary building code requirements. To achieve these objectives the Johnstones developed a number of innovative features; in all, they filed about thirty patents and partial patents. The most significant was for what Johnstone calls the "swivel"—a central connection device located at the bottom of the main column that links fixed pipes and wiring from the ground to those aboard the rotating superstructure. The swivel allows the latter to turn indefinitely. Johnstone calls rotating designs without this capability—structures that need to be reversed to unwind connections or dump waste water—"RVs on a stick."[47]

Construction began in June 2001 and by August, when the central steel column that would house the elevator and the rotating connections was in place, the neighbors knew that no ordinary house was going up next door. Constructed by the Johnstones and a varying team of two to six workers, the house gradually took shape. The stationary lower section with stucco-covered concrete block walls features a garage (with twin car turntables in the floor) and an adaptable space that can function as a playroom and guest quarters. The steel-framed superstructure above is 80 feet in diameter. Its floor-to-ceiling glass walls enclose the house's primary living space.

A self-described "techno-freak," Johnstone integrated into his house an array of home automation features. It is a perfect representative of the wave of new residential designs that came to be called "smart houses." Facilitated by the rise of the personal computer in the 1990s, these homes were crammed with every conceivable gadget, some one-off inventions, others just entering the market.[48] The goal was twofold: increased efficiency and greater ease and comfort. The latter captured more popular attention, as homeowners, manufacturers, and computer and housing research centers vied for the most advanced yet carefree dwelling.

The high-tech theme of the Johnstone house extends beyond individual gadgets. The entire structure was conceived as a centralized collection of systems, and a main computer is used to regulate all aspects of the interior environment, from rotational speed and direction to lighting, temperature, and access. Responding to voice commands or handheld units, the system identifies the owner of the voice and calls up preset temperature and lighting preferences for that individual. The elevator planned for the central shaft will open to selected individuals via a biometric fingerprint reader.

As Al and Janet Johnstone became further immersed in their revolving house project they had two insights. First, the concept elicited an enormous amount of popular interest, from TV news programs and documentaries to newspaper and magazine articles

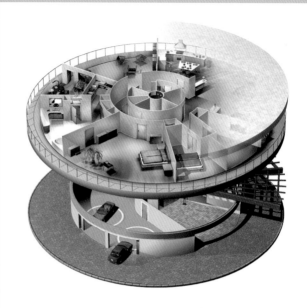

TOP LEFT: Johnstone House steel framework
TOP RIGHT: Johnstone House cutaway
LEFT: Johnstone House, 2006
ABOVE: Johnstone's patented swivel, where
all ground pipes and lines connect with
the rotation portion of the house, allowing the
house to rotate 360 degrees continually.

Johnstone House, 2007

to the regular "knock on the door request for a tour."[49] Second, as they worked out the myriad details of building their unconventional house they were developing an expertise that would be valuable if a curious public could be converted into customers. Other designers who developed rotating houses for their own use in the late twentieth century had come to the same conclusion. Recognizing the promotional potential in their homes these inventors became entrepreneurs and made arrangements with appliance, electronic, and building product manufacturers who provided hot tubs, toasters, TVs, and installations from floor tiles to faucets to light fixtures in exchange for a place on the house's website and a mention in the media coverage.

With varying degrees of commitment and varying degrees of subsequent success these inventors established companies that offered to assist others interested in building their own rotating house. Johnstone said, "I built the home for us and I put a lot of work into its design. If I can sell that experience it would be great, but if not, that's fine too."[50] Johnstone sells his patented "swivel"—the two-ton assembly of connectors and joints that sits at the base of the house and allows it to turn 360-degrees indefinitely. He also offers consulting services to assist in navigating building-code issues and selecting and installing the smart-house apparatus.

Some companies offer just technical assistance, others sell complete homes in prefabricated packages. One of the first companies to successfully market and sell a rotating house was Domespace Homes of

Johnstone House, 2007

Scaer, France. Patrick Marsilli established the firm in 1989 after designing and building a rotating home for his family. Promotional materials liken Marsilli's house to an igloo or traditional African hut, however, the exposed convex underside lends the structure a shape more akin to a flying saucer. The design uses an arching framework of glue-laminated wood beams to support wood sheathing and shingles. When Marsilli decided to manufacture and market copies of his design, he developed a kit that included prefabricated beams and all the other wood components, which are manufactured at a plant in the Czech Republic before delivery to the building site. At present the company has established joint ventures and

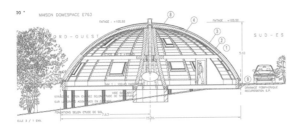

TOP: Domespace
Home section
ABOVE: Domespace
glue-laminated
framing

distributorships throughout France, as well as in Switzerland, the Czech Republic, Denmark, and the United States. Over the last twenty-five years Domespace has sold more than one hundred rotating homes.[51]

Similar, though smaller-scale, companies in Canada, Germany, and Australia manufacture rotating house kits or consult on one-off rotating projects. In 2000 Don Dunick designed his own polygonal rotating house in New Zealand that has an exterior form notably similar to George Fred Keck's 1934

House of Tomorrow. Dunick partnered with a home building firm to establish a new company in Australia called LightHouse Projects that offers three different models of pre-engineered steel-and-glass rotating houses. Luke Everingham, an Australian acoustical engineer, finished a rotating house of his own design for his family in 2006 that is more vernacular in styling than Dunick's version. Everingham's octagonal house has a facade made largely of glass windows and doors, but a hipped roof, deep overhang, and wraparound wood veranda that reference traditional ranch detailing more than a high-tech futurism.[52] Today Everingham offers his services supervising the design and construction of similar houses. In Heuchelheim, Germany, architect Heinrich Rinn's company Rinn-Dreh-Haus markets the design and construction of rotating houses and other structures based upon Rinn's own timber-frame rotating house.

After a century of experimentation, unrealized plans, and one-of-a-kind constructions, the appearance of these companies suggests that the twenty-first century may still see the idea of a rotating house win broader popularity. The flood of media coverage these projects have received confirms widespread interest. The concept of a responsive architecture that is naturally efficient dovetails neatly with other contemporary building trends such as smart and green design. Yet the number of built projects these companies have completed remains negligible. As the world continues to rapidly urbanize, perhaps inventors and entrepreneurs will have better luck with high-rise buildings rather than single family homes.

TOP: Domespace Home model
LEFT: Living room and kitchen of
Domespace Home

LEFT: Don Dunick's LightHouse Projects model
RIGHT: LightHouse Projects kitchen

Luke Everingham's Rotating House, 2006

Kan-iti Hotel, Atami
Japan, ca. 1955

Revolving High-Rises

This book opened with a discussion of George Ade's idea for a rotating apartment building in New York that would take advantage of weather conditions and views in every direction. Beginning in the postwar era, such ideas were increasingly given serious consideration. As prime land grew more valuable in city centers and resort areas, pushing construction upward, developers looked for new ways to capitalize on the value of small lots.

The Kan-iti Hotel, constructed in the Japanese resort community of Atami in the mid-1950s, demonstrates one approach to rotating high-rise design.[53] On top of the five-story modern building there was an additional cylindrical level that rotated once per hour. The rotating section's exterior had operable windows running around its circumference, while the interior was divided into eight separate guest rooms. As it turned, the view from each of the rooms would cycle from the harbor on one side to the city and mountains on the other. Guests reached the revolving section either by an interior circular stairway or an elevator that ran within a glazed elevator shaft attached to the side of the building. Though only a small-scale application, the Kan-iti's rotating rooms provided a premium attraction that undoubtedly drew higher rates. The hotel, with a flying saucer–like structure on the roof, foreshadowed the hundreds of revolving-restaurant-on-hotel designs that would appear around the world in the following decades.

In 1962 a real estate developer hired Richmond, Virginia, architect Haigh Jamgochian to design a hotel and marina complex for oceanfront property in Virginia Beach. The client was looking for a concept that would draw attention to the hotel and ensure steady occupancy. Jamgochian proposed a pair of twenty-story towers, each level of which featured six wedge-shaped rooms cantilevered out from a central shaft. To guarantee that the design would generate interest, the architect planned for both towers to turn. Unlike most rotating structures conceived in the past, the towers were to move without the use of rollers, wheels, or bearings. Instead, the central columns would float on a thin layer of hydraulic fluid and would move by hydraulic pressure.

Jamgochian called his design the Revolving Tree House. It was one of a series of bold, futuristic towers developed by the architect in the early 1960s, all of which shared flower-shaped plans with central stationary cores and apartment units extending outward like petals. Photos of the Revolving Tree House models made it onto the Associated Press wire and were published widely. But when the time came to move forward, his client backed out. It wasn't a

Haigh Jamgochian with a model of his
Revolving Tree House, 1962

surprising turn of events; almost all of Jamgochian's projects have ended similarly. Years later the architect explained why his unorthodox designs rarely made it past the proposal stage: "people are used to doing what they're used to doing. They want to be one of the Joneses and they don't want to be pointed out."[54]

Looking back upon his Revolving Tree House design forty-four years later, Haigh Jamgochian remains convinced that it was a good idea. He also felt that the benefits of a rotating design extended beyond just attracting attention, or controlling the sun and the views. He described how his paired towers would rotate at slightly different rates so that the visitors in the rooms would see different visitors while they rotated through-out their stay. He said, "as the buildings moved people would wave at each other, like people do from a passing train or ship. And I think if people wave more they'd get along better with each other."[55]

Rolf Disch, designer of the Heliotrop House, adapted his rotating design in the latter 1990s for a hotel to be constructed in the Swiss Alps. The hotel design was to be between six and eleven stories tall and would feature fifteen wedge-shaped guest rooms extending from the central column's elevator lobby and spiral staircase. The main exterior differences between the house and hotel (other than their scale) were that the latter had a glass walled lobby on the ground floor and a framework of diagonal braces surrounding the entire structure.[56] Thus far, nothing has come of the project. Disch said that after the first designs he did not pursue the idea and moved on to new commissions.[57]

Postwar designers also looked to apply rotating technology to high-rise apartment buildings. In 1965, a large project featuring nine rotating apartment towers ranging in height between eighteen and twenty-four stories was planned for beachfront property in La Jolla, California, near San Diego. (It was this design that Al Johnstone recalled when considering building his own rotating house thirty-five years later.) The property owner claimed that ocean views commanded a $25,000 premium over those facing east. Ultimately the local land-use board rejected plans for the project.[58]

Another unrealized scheme proposed in the 1980s was for a 900-foot-tall apartment tower named Eclipse, to be built on a promi-nent site overlooking Sydney Harbour in Australia.[59] The design called for an ellipse-shaped superstructure wrapped around a fixed cylindrical core. Eclipse was to make a complete revolution every day, always keep-ing a narrow edge pointed toward the sun to reduce insulation and air-conditioning costs. At night the tower would be "parked" in an east/west direction. The goal of the project, designed by Tony Pegrum of the Hassell Group, was to develop a signature structure that complemented the high-profile location while taking maximum advantage of the sur-rounding views—of the harbor, Sydney Opera House, and Harbour Bridge—from within the units.

While earlier attempts never got far, a Brazilian company constructed the first fully revolving high-rise apartment building in 2004. Called Suite Vollard, the eleven-story structure was designed by Bruno De Franco and built by Design Essentials SA in Curitiba, a major city in the south of the country. The building is primarily cylindrical in shape with a rectilinear block running the height of the tower on one side. Each apartment unit occupies an entire floor. Residents can control the speed and direction of rotation of their apartment independent of the other floors. The exterior walls of the cylindrical section are fully glazed and have open balconies extending around the circumference. The primary living space of each apartment—dining room, living room, bedroom, and office—is contained within the circular plan. A ring-type turntable rotates the primary living space around a stationary core that includes all the plumbing, electricity, and HVAC connections. This configuration, similar to that employed in revolving restaurants, permits the use of conventional fixtures and connectors. Like the center core, the elevator tower does not revolve.

Suite Vollard's owners see it as a concept building to test the idea, attract potential tenants, and demonstrate to other real estate entrepreneurs that it could be accomplished. Carrousel Buildings Technology Management Company, based in Fort Walton Beach, Florida, offers developer clients the services of their team of architects, construction specialists, and engineers. According to the company's promotional material, the basic concept is highly adaptable: to fit a client's needs and budget, floors can be added to the design, or subtracted, and additional towers can be connected to form larger complexes. The company is establishing the legal and financial infrastructure to enable the construction of more Suite Vollards, but at present, the tower in Curitiba is one of a kind.

TOP: Computer rendering of proposed double revolving tower based on Suite Vollard
LEFT: Suite Vollard

Suite Vollard is unlikely to retain its unique title for long. As this book goes to press there are three projects for revolving apartment buildings currently planned, all to be constructed in the United Arab Emirates city Dubai. The country's ruler, Sheikh Mohammed bin Rashid Al Maktoum, eager to diversify UAE's economy, has spurred an enormous real estate boom in the city. Artificial peninsula and archipelagos have been built, along with hundreds of new buildings. Dubai has become a center of architectural immodesty, featuring distinctive designs like the Burj Al Arab, the world's tallest freestanding hotel, and the Burj Dubai Tower, which is intended to be the tallest structure in the world when completed.

Plans for the Rotating Residences project by High Rise Properties show a circular twelve-story form with stepped terraces running along the exterior. It narrows near the top to incorporate four rotating penthouses and a two-story rotating villa. On a larger scale, the developer Dubai Property Ring is planning a thirty-story 200-unit apartment building called Time Residences. The entire 88,000-ton cylindrical structure will rotate once per week, powered by solar energy. Descriptions of the tower note that the developer plans to build twenty-three more rotating towers, one in each of the world's time zones.[60]

Perhaps the most ambitious project is the Dynamic Architecture Tower, designed by Italian-Israeli architect David Fisher. Like the Suite Vollard in Curitiba, each floor will rotate independently, but while the former has a single residential unit on each floor, most of the sixty-eight floors on Fisher's design will contain multiple apartments.[61] Several features will make the Dynamic Architecture Tower unique among other rotating high-rise designs. Because floor plans are oblong rather than circular, the structure's form will change as it rotates. By sychronizing the movement of the floors the exterior as a whole can gently writhe and twist itself into a variety of configurations. Fisher expects that horizontal turbines inserted in narrow gaps between each floor and rooftop solar panels will provide more power than the entire building requires. Most of the structure will be prefabricated as a series of modules that will be shipped to the site and raised by crane. The permanent prefabrication factory will then supply modules for similar towers planned for Moscow and other cities.

David Fisher recalled that he came up with the idea while shopping for a condo in Miami Beach and New York City. Struck by the disparity in prices between units with more or less dramatic vistas he thought, "why can't we rotate a whole damn building around so everyone can have a view?"[62] The Dynamic Architecture Tower and the other rotating designs planned for Dubai are up-to-date interpretations of George Ade's dream, and the dreams of all the other rotating residence designers from the past century. If these towers are constructed and prove to be more than cutting-edge curiosities accessible to only the super rich, if they are repeated in other cities around the world, they will further the exploration of designs that are flexible, dynamic, and responsive to the needs of their occupants.

David Fisher's Dynamic Architecture Tower

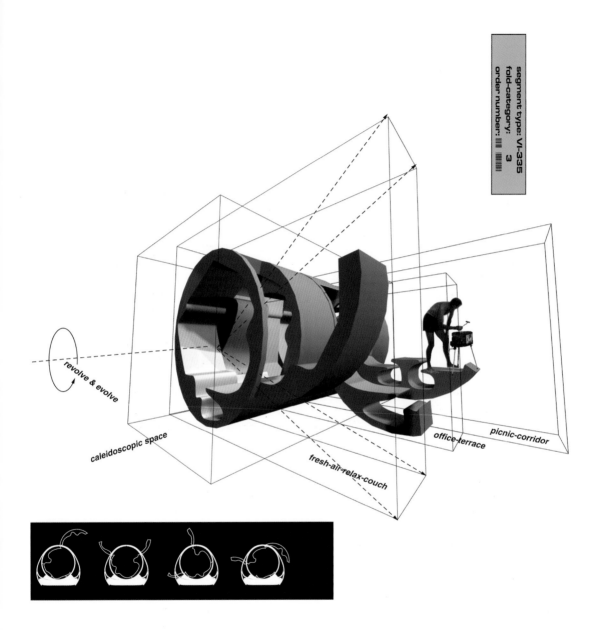

revolve & evolve

caleidoscopic space

fresh-air-relax-couch

office-terrace

picnic-corridor

Conceptual rendering of the turnOn living unit
showing how modules open to the outside

CONCLUSION

The rotating structures and devices developed over the preceding centuries have shared one general characteristic: all turned on an upright, vertical axis. House and apartment designers, theater architects, jail designers, and others, all saw this prevailing model as an appropriate means of employing rotation to help meet their needs. While walls were made to move and views made to change, up remained up and down was still down.

But recently one group of designers has departed from this established orientation seeking new ways of utilizing rotation. In 2001, the Austrian design firm AllesWirdGut (German for "everything will go well") developed a modular living space called turnOn for an exhibition on innovative housing.[1] The design is made up of a varying number of rotatable, wheel-like modules, linked together and oriented longitudinally. Each molded plastic module contains a different set of furnishings linked to different activities or functions. For example, one wheel may feature a dining table, another a bed. Throughout a day spent living in turnOn, the occupant would rotate each module to present a suitable combination of those portions of the different modules needed for whatever they were doing at the moment.

AWG's turnOn is a critique of rectilinear, one-off residential design with rooms and furniture inflexibly zoned for specific functions. Inspired by the automobile industry, its interior is mass-producible—with undulating and sensual curves blending one into the next. The line between floor, ceiling, and wall is intentionally blurred, suggesting an environment more suitable for zero gravity. In fact, the designers also attributed their inspiration to scenes from the film *2001: A Space Odyssey*. While more concept than livable space, its designers do feel there are opportunities to incorporate elements of turnOn into more conventional housing. Like the turntable-based internally rotating designs, AllesWirdGut's turnOn strives for a more efficient use of space and the empowerment of occupants to reconfigure their living areas based on the needs of the moment. Is this the future of rotating design? Or will the idea be shelved as a quirky concept that is both intriguing and somewhat unsettling?

For well over a century the designers of rotating houses and other building forms considered the widespread adoption of their ideas on the immediate horizon. Newspaper editors, authors, and filmmakers also espoused this vision, even if expressing reservations about the changes that would

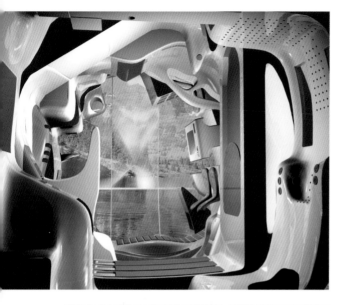

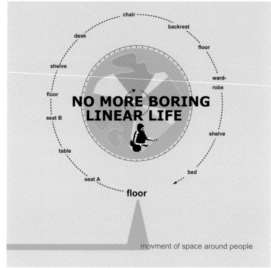

accompany this seemingly inevitable revolution in architecture. But except for the revolving restaurant boom of the 1960s and '70s and the limited success of revolving house manufacturers in recent years, revolving architecture remains a fringe trend. Its popularization remains elusive.

Though he first conceived of the design in the 1980s and the first company passed on placing it in production, Luigi Colani still has big expectations for his Rotor Haus. He is hoping to build his EcoCity, featuring 15,000 Rotor Hauses on the island of Chongming in China. Current plans are to adapt his original design setting the fiberglass interior within an aluminum structure and exterior skin. The house will be sectional, prefabricated as two main pieces that can be easily transported and bolted together at the building site. Domespace Homes, Light-House Projects, and other manufacturers and entrepreneurs have offices and distributors ready to serve an upswing in customers seeking a rotating residence.

While inventors and entrepreneurs look toward the future and continue their efforts to develop new livable, affordable, and popularly acceptable rotating structures, several designs from the last century remain to offer examples of how those in the past met the challenge of getting a building to turn. Though their number is relatively small, they form a body of completed designs that show the concept is not a gimmick, and that the problems of rotation are not insurmountable, at least technically.

Today, Angelo Invernizzi's Villa Girasole survives, worn but largely unchanged from its original appearance. The house last rotated

TOP: turnOn interior
BOTTOM: AllesWirdGut's conceptual basis for turnOn

in 2002. Uneven ground settlement has pushed it out of plumb, so that the center column now leans against one side of the tower chamber. In 2003 Lidia and Lino Invernizzi donated the house and grounds to the Swiss Accademia di Architettura and the Archivio del Moderno di Mendrisio. Current plans call for rehabilitating the building, getting it rotating again, and converting it to an educational center focusing on the restoration of modern architecture.

The D'Angelo house in Snow Creek, which Bill Butler painstakingly restored in the early 2000s, is often included in architectural tours of the Palm Springs area. The Wilson house on Blakely Island also survives essentially intact. The exterior of Richard Foster's house in Wilton, Connecticut, is unchanged from its 1960s appearance. In 2003 it was extensively remodeled on the interior; only the hexagonal floor tiles in the central stationary core and the spiral staircase are original.

Revolving treatment cottages at sanatoria were demolished or sold off when antibiotics proved a more effective cure than sunlight and fresh air. Some were moved to the seashore, where they were rented by the hour to beachgoers. Historic rotating summer houses can still be found in their original garden locations or in salvage yards throughout Britain; new prefab models can still be purchased by at least one firm that sold them a century ago. Of the approximately eighteen rotating jails constructed in the late 1800s, two exist today. Both the "Old Jail" in Crawfordsville, Indiana, and the "Squirrel Cage Jail" in Council Bluffs, Iowa, are now museums. Postwar auditoriums in Český

Krumlov and Tampere have been altered over time, but continue to provide dynamic summer theater experiences in the open air.

The first generation of revolving restaurants generally did not fare well. The iconic symbolism of host towers and their telecommunication function have made some military targets. London's Top of the Tower restaurant was closed to all but private functions in 1980, a decade after the tower suffered an IRA bomb attack. The revolving restaurant atop the Hillbrow Tower in Johannesburg, South Africa, was closed in 1981 after only a decade of operation due to concerns it too would be attacked by political guerillas.[2] John Graham's Le Ronde in Honolulu closed in the late 1980s. In Germany, the Fernmeldeturm revolving restaurant in Nuremberg has been closed for over a decade. The Europaturm restaurant in Frankfurt was closed in 1999. Hamburg's Heinrich-Hertz-Turm restaurant closed in 2001 due to asbestos contamination and changes in building and fire codes. The restaurant atop the Henninger brewery silo was closed in 2003.

A number of revolving restaurants survive, but no longer rotate. Sometimes when machinery broke down it was not fixed and the restaurant was either closed, was reused for other purposes, or continued in operation as a conventional stationary restaurant. To the owners repair and ongoing maintenance costs were no longer justified by the reduced appeal of this feature among customers. The 1964 Circle One restaurant atop the Baltimore, Maryland, Holiday Inn, for example, was converted to meeting space in the 1980s when the rotating mechanism failed.

Holiday Inn,
Baltimore, Maryland

The decision to abandon Circle One's machinery was made easier by the fact that the view out the restaurant's windows had been diminished over the years by taller adjacent construction. This was not an uncommon situation for early revolving restaurants. When first built, the host structure may have been among the tallest in the area, with a view looking down on the city below. Over time, though, as new buildings rose above the restaurant, the view often closed in and became that of adjacent offices and apartments, rather than rooftops and a distant horizon. In other cases the view was problematic not because it was gradually filled in but because it was considered inappropriate. According to a historian of the Saudi Arabian royal family, the revolving restaurant on top of the 1970 Riyadh Water Tower was closed because its view included the private garden of King Faisal's favorite sister.[3]

In the late 1990s, Piz Gloria in Switzerland underwent a redesign that included converting the heliport to a permanent deck area and expanding the dining room to accommodate additional patrons.

While the exterior still resembles Bloefeld's mountaintop lair, the only interior feature recognizable from the film is a decorative metal screen alongside the stairway. A trip today to Berlin's Telecafé would be familiar to anyone who had visited the restaurant in the 1960s. The futuristic entrance hall, including the stylized baluster panels and the doors, survives, although the once-colorful interior was recently painted a bland white. The round elevator lobby in the tower base is completely intact. In the restaurant itself, the dimensions and layout remain unchanged, as does the glass block mural at the entrance.

Confirming a generally fading popularity in the United States, the last revolving restaurant constructed in the United States was the 1996 Stratosphere Tower in Las Vegas. Though the revolving restaurant's heyday has passed in the West, it still has devotees. In 1994 Clarence Reed, an Atlanta, Georgia, computer salesman undertook a well-publicized personal quest to visit every revolving restaurant in the United States. Ten years later he had dined at all forty-nine restaurants in existence at the time.[4] One informal measure of the concept's enduring affection is its appearance on internet photo-sharing sites like Flickr, where a search turns up over 1,200 photographs of revolving restaurants worldwide. Most are personal snapshots showing couples, friends, families, and business associates gathered to dine, drink, and enjoy the view. Online photos confirm that revolving restaurants remain common tourist destinations, as well as preferred sites for dates, weddings, product launches, and business meetings. In East Asia and the Middle East, where the construction of new revolving restaurant designs continues, these establishments remain a potent symbol of progress and pride.

As time draws the American and European revolving restaurant boom into a more distant past, the first generation of revolving restaurants have begun to attract the attention of governmental heritage offices. Seattle's Space Needle was listed as a city historic landmark in 1999. Four years later the conservation agency English Heritage listed London's Post Office Tower as a Grade II building, designating it "extremely important" and making it eligible for funding for restoration work. Arts minister Baroness Blackstone noted that the tower, "is an icon for sixties design and science, and we should be proud of it."[5]

Throughout the first decades of experimentation, rotating building designers contended with a range of technical challenges. They worked their way through complicated systems of connections to bring services into the building. Designers were able to fill the houses with the typical appointments only by resorting to elaborate joints, trenches, and storage tanks. Externally rotating designs featured wedge-shaped rooms to take full advantage of the interior space. These factors were probably enough to temper the curiosity of other inventors or architects interested in giving the idea a try, as well as any potential homebuyers.

Today, the technological hurdles of rotating architecture have largely been overcome. Al and Janet Johnstone's swivel enables houses and other structures to turn continuously while meeting all the requirements of a conventional home. While the initial costs of a rotating house are typically higher than a conventional construction, designers claim that these costs can be recouped through increased energy efficiency. With the current interest in green design, smart homes, and distinctive high-rise homes, it would seem that (as with the dawn of the twentieth century and the beginning of the postwar era) the rotating residence is an idea whose time has come.

Despite these steps forward rotating building designers still find there is greater interest in the idea than there are customers willing to put down deposits. Several clear challenges still inhibit the wider adoption of rotating residences. First, local planning and zoning regulations and officials are ill-equipped to deal with the new variables of rotating designs. Second, companies have had a hard time securing financing for their potential customers when there are few comparables and no established proof of resale value. The greatest remaining difficulty, however, is surely a continuing ambivalence on the part of the public over the basic concept of rotating architecture. Stories in popular culture abound of occupants losing control of runaway rotating houses that, in their ability to move, also seemed to acquire a degree of cognizance and will. They were common reactions throughout history whenever society confronted a new technology. In the past people generally were not willing to reconsider their assumptions about what a home is to do and not do. The question for designers of rotating buildings today is whether those assumptions are as immovable as a traditional structure on a fixed foundation.

NOTES

INTRODUCTION

1 George Ade, "Life on the Ocean Wave," *Washington Post*, March 25, 1906, SM3.

2 A similar turntable altar was constructed in 1953 at the Chapel of the Four Chaplains at Temple University in Philadelphia. More recent versions were built at the National Institutes of Health in Bethesda, Maryland, and at U.S. military bases such as the one at Guantanamo, Cuba.

3 Quoted in Patricia Brooks, "Rotating View and Versatile Menu," *New York Times*, August 3, 1986, CN21.

4 Don DeLillo, *Cosmopolis: A Novel* (New York: Scribner, 2003), 5.

5 William Zuk and Roger H. Clark, *Kinetic Architecture* (New York: Van Nostrand Reinhold, 1970).

6 Wolfgang Schivelbusch, *The Railway Journey: The Industrialization and Perception of Time and Space* (Berkeley: University of California Press), 1987.

7 Alan Trachtenberg, foreword to *The Railway Journey*, by Wolfgang Schivelbusch, xv.

CHAPTER ONE

1 C. Suetonius Tranquillus, *The Lives of the Twelve Caesars*, ed. Alexander Thomson, 360 (London: George Bell and Sons, 1893). For a review of the history of painted skies on domes and ceilings see Chapter x, "Ceilings Like the Sky," in William Richard Lethaby, *Architecture, Mysticism, and Myth* (1891; repr., New York: Cosimo, 2005).

2 David Hemsoll, "Reconstructing the Octagonal Dining Room of Nero's Golden House," *Architectural History* 32 (1989): 10.

3 Axel Boethius, *The Golden House of Nero: Some Aspects of Roman Architecture* (Ann Arbor: University of Michigan Press, 1960), 117. Larry F. Ball suggests this is most likely, that the revolving room, if it existed, was probably located in a more prominent area of the Domus Aurea site such as the Palatine. Larry F. Ball, email to the author, May 20, 2007.

4 Quoted in Rosemarie Haag Bletter, "The Interpretation of the Glass Dream—Expressionist Architecture and the History of the Crystal Metaphor," *Journal of the Society of Architectural Historians* 40, no. 1 (1981): 20–43.

5 T. K. Derry and Trevor Illtyd Williams, *A Short History of Technology from the Earliest Times to AD 1900* (Oxford: Clarendon Press, 1960), 75.

6 Richard Leslie Hills, *Power from Wind: A History of Windmill Technology* (New York: Cambridge University Press, 1994), 42.

7 Ladislao Reti, "Leonardo and Ramelli," *Technology and Culture* 13, no. 4 (1972): 578. Leonardo's epicyclic gear is in folio 112r, Codex Madrid I. Ramelli's bookcase is featured in his book *Le diverse et Artificiose Machine del Capitano Agostina Ramelli* (Paris: A Parigi, 1588).

8 Antonio Averlino Filarete and John Richard Spencer, *Treatise on Architecture* (New Haven: Yale University Press, 1965), book XXI, folios 171v and 172r.

9 Arnold A. Putnam, "The Introduction of the Revolving Turret," *American Neptune* 56, no. 2 (1986): 117.

10 "The Revolving Tower and Its Inventor," *Harper's New Monthly Magazine*, January 1863, 241.

11 James L. Nelson, *Reign of Iron: The Story of the First Battling Ironclads, the Monitor and the Merrimack* (New York: Harper Paperbacks, 2005), 267. The author of the cited quote was Lieutenant James H. Rochelle.

12 Putnam, "The Introduction of the Revolving Turret," 119.

13 Rudy Rolf, "Revolving Concrete Turrets" *Fort* (Liverpool: Fortress Study Group, 1988), 119–29.

14 Scott Cooper, "Ornamental Structures in Medieval Gardens," *Proceedings of the Society of Antiquarians of Scotland* 129 (1999): 817–39.

15 Anne Hagopian Van Buren, "The Park of Hesdin," in *Ornamental Structures in the Medieval Gardens of Scotland,* ed. Scott Cooper, 124

(Edinburgh: Royal Museum of Scotland, 1999). The park also featured animated carved wood statues including a group of monkeys covered in fur and attached to a bridge. As guests arrived the marionette monkeys were made to nod and wave using pullied hoists, levers, and hydraulic systems.

16 Derek Hudson, *Kensington Palace* (London: Peter Davies, 1968), 42.

17 Isaac Disraeli and Benjamin Disraeli, *Curiosities of Literature* (New York: Veazie Hurd and Houghton, 1864), 385.

18 Augustus Jessopp, "The Elders of Arcady," *Living Age* 226 (1900): 127.

19 Ibid.

20 Paul Kuritz, *The Making of Theatre History* (Englewood Cliffs, NJ: Prentice Hall, 1988), 114.

21 A. C. Scott, *The Kabuki Theatre of Japan* (Mineola, NY: Dover, 1999), 282.

22 "General Mention," *New York Times*, December 4, 1884, 4.

23 "We, Us & Company At Mud Springs," Grand Opera House Programme, Grand Opera House, Cincinnati, OH, September 20, 1885.

24 "We, Us & Co.," *Atlanta Constitution*, November 29, 1886, 7.

25 "The Lounger," *The Critic: A Weekly Review of Literature and the Arts* 12 (1889): 19. Barnard and Mestayer and his company had a hit with *We, Us & Co*. Positive reviews indicate it played through-out the eastern half of the United States between 1884 and at least 1886. According to a playbill from a performance at the Grand Opera House in Cincinnati, Ohio, the revolving house was patented on January 29, 1884, but no record of such a patent can be found—suggesting that the reference was part of the gag. That the building was turned by windlass and mule is mentioned in a description

of a later revolving house. See "A Revolving House," *New York Times*, July 8, 1908, 6.

26 Wendell Cole, "America's First Revolving Stage," *Western Speech*, Winter 1963, 36.

27 Letter from John Charles Haugh, February 7, 1985, Montgomery County Cultural Foundation files.

28 Earl Bruce White, *The Rotary Jail Revisited*, undated manuscript, 2.

29 Pauly Catalog, quoted in White, *The Rotary Jail Revisited*, 7.

30 Walter A. Lunden, "The Rotary Jail, Or Human Squirrel Cage," *Journal of the Society of Architectural Historians* 18, no. 4 (1959): 155. McGaughey cites an unpublished article by A. H. White, a former employee of Pauly Jail Company.

31 Tamara Hemmerlein, Executive Director, Montgomery County Cultural Foundation and Old Jail Museum, in discussion with the author, July 2006.

32 Alfred Hopkins, *Prisons and Prison Building* (New York: Architectural Book Publishing Co., 1930), 218.

33 Robin Evans, *The Fabrication of Virtue: English Prison Architecture, 1750–1840* (New York: Cambridge University Press, 1982), 218.

34 See Michel Foucault, *Discipline and Punish: The Birth of the Prison*, translated by Alan Sheridan (New York: Pantheon, 1977).

35 Lunden, "The Rotary Jail," 156.

36 Stephan Oettermann, *The Panorama, History of a Mass Medium* (New York: Zone Books, 1997), 325.

37 Oettermann, *The Panorama, History of a Mass Medium*, 31.

38 Alec McEwen, "Revolving Observation Towers," *Yarmouth Archaeology* (1995), 33.

39 A. Boomer, "Whirligig Ruin Wrought By a Revolving House,"

Boston Daily Globe, February 9, 1890, 24.

40 Dudley Blanchard, "Tornado Proof Building," U.S. Patent 439,376, filed July 30, 1890, and issued on October 28, 1890. Blanchard mentions in the patent that his design, "is especially adapted for use as a hospital or as a hospital adjunct…so as to present the sick-room to the sunshine during the whole of a long summer day, or to turn it so as to be in the shade all day, or to present the rooms to receive the wind directly through in any desired manner." Blanchard's design was subsequently published in French newspapers and reference to those articles was made in several US publications.

41 J. Ross Browne, *Yusef: Or, the Journey of the Frangi: a Crusade in the East* (New York: Arno Press, 1977), 28. Another traveler from the same period noted that in Spain such "revolving baby-holders" were specifically designed to only accommodate infants in order to prevent abandonment of four- and five-year-olds. See Charles Rockwell, *Sketches of Foreign Travel, and Life At Sea* (New York: Dennet D. Appleton, 1842), 239.

42 Silvio A. Bedini, *Jefferson and Science* (Chapel Hill: University of North Carolina Press, 2002), 72. Jefferson developed numerous other contrivances that enabled him to be served while remaining separated from those serving him, including vertical dumbwaiters and an earth closet that could be emptied in the basement. See Dell Upton, *Architecture in the United States* (New York: Oxford University Press, 1998), 30.

43 Elizabeth E. Howell. Self Waiting Table. US Patent 464,073, filed September 14, 1891, and issued December 1, 1891. Christine Frederick referred to the device as "the silent waitress" in her book *The New Housekeeping: Efficiency Studies in Home Management* (New York: Doubleday, Page, 1914), 80.

44 Robida, *The Twentieth Century* (1883; repr. , Middletown, CT: Wesleyan University Press, 2004) 62.

CHAPTER TWO

1 Buster Keaton's 1922 film *The Electric House* lampooned this trend of household gadgetry with its operable bookshelves, automatic lazy Susans, and a bathtub that slides between the bathroom and bedroom on a concealed track all controlled by wall-mounted switches and dials. *The Electric House*, DVD (1922; Synergy Entertainment, 2007).

2 Le Corbusier, *Towards a New Architecture* (New York: Praeger, 1970), 89, 23.

3 Charles DeKay, "Primitive Homes," *American Architect & Building News* 94 (1908): 119.

4 Leslie G. Goat, "Housing the Horseless Carriage: America's Early Private Garages" in *Perspectives in Vernacular Architecture, III*, eds. Thomas Carter and Bernard L. Herman, 64 (Columbia: University of Missouri Press, 1989). Early cars either lacked a reverse gear entirely or were difficult to maneuver in reverse. They also had wider turning radii than the horse-drawn carriages they replaced. Existing driveways and porte cocheres were often ill-equipped to accommodate automobiles.

5 Norman Bel Geddes, *Horizons* (Boston: Little, Brown, 1932), 105.

6 Glenn Porter and Raymond Loewy, *Raymond Loewy: Designs for a Consumer Culture* (Wilmington, DE: Hagley Museum and Library, 2002), 38.

7 Bel Geddes, *Horizons*, 107.

8 Thomas Parke Hughes, a leading scholar of the social construction of technology, notes that professional inventors are also motivated by the pure pleasure of problem solving. "The challenge of sweet problems that have foiled numerous others often stimulates the independents' problem choices. They believe their special gifts will bring success where others have failed. Not strongly motivated by a defined need, they exhibit an elementary joy in problem solving as an end in itself." Thomas Parke Hughes, "The Evolution of Large Technological Systems," in *The Social Construction of Technological Systems: New Directions in the Sociology and History of Technology*, ed. Wiebe E. Bijker, Thomas P. Hughes, Trevor J. Pinch, 61 (Cambridge, MA: MIT Press, 1987).

9 A. Boomer, "Whirligig Ruin Wrought By a Revolving House," *Boston Daily Globe*, February 9, 1890, 24.

10 Huntly Carter, *The Theatre of Max Reinhardt* (New York: Mitchel Kennerley, 1914), 150.

11 Amy S. Green, *The Revisionist Stage: American Directors Reinvent the Classics* (New York: Cambridge University Press, 1994), 19.

12 Quoted in Wendell Cole, "America's First Revolving Stage," *Western Speech*, Winter 1963, 37.

13 Arnold Aronson, "Theaters of the Future," *Theatre Journal* 33, no. 4 (December 1981), 495.

14 "A House that Turns with the Sun," *Scientific American* 89, no. 19 (1903): 330. Though drawings show a bathtub and toilet in one of the upper-floor bedrooms, descriptions of the house provide little information about the means used to make plumbing and other connections, saying only, "a central apparatus, above which

the house turns, allows the introduction of water, of gas, of electricity, as well as the exit of water, etc."

15 "Houses Now on Rotary Platforms," *New York Times*, September 25, 1904, 33.

16 Jean Saidman, Rotary Structure for Treating Patients with Solar and other Actinic Lights. Patent GB353,266 (FR680179), filed August 1, 1930, and issued on July 23, 1931.

17 Thierry Lefebvre and Cécile Raynal, "Le Solarium Tournant d'Aix-les-Bains," *La Revue du Praticien* 56 (December 15, 2006): 2200.

18 Margaret Campbell, "What Tuberculosis Did for Modernism: The Influence of a Curative Environment on Modernist Design and Architecture," *Medical History*, 49 no. 4 (October 1, 2005): 470.

19 Cosmo Hamilton, *Confession: A Novel* (Garden City, NY: Doubleday, 1926).

20 Campbell, "What Tuberculosis Did for Modernism," 470.

21 Thomas Carrington, *Fresh Air and How to Use It* (New York: National Association for the Study and Prevention of Tuberculosis, 1914), 160.

22 "Push Button, Get Sun," *Washington Post*, June 5, 1911, 2.

23 Ibid.

24 Ibid.

25 Such attributes would be of primary importance when revolving mechanisms were introduced into future designs for permanent homes and restaurants.

26 "Push Button, Get Sun," 2.

27 National Trust, "Shaw's Corner," http://www.nationaltrust.org.uk/main/w-vh/w-visits/w-findaplace/w-shawscorner/w-shawscorner-garden/w-shawscorner-garden-hut.htm (accessed June 19, 2007).

28 Bruno Taut, "The Rotating House,"

Stadtbaukunst-Frühlicht 2 (1920): 31.

29 Rosemarie Haag Bletter, "The Interpretation of the Glass Dream—Expressionist Architecture and the History of the Crystal Metaphor," *Journal of the Society of Architectural Historians* XL, no. 1 (1981): 20–43.

30 John Milner, *Vladimir Tatlin and the Russian Avant-Garde* (New Haven: Yale University Press, 1983), 164.

31 "Life, Letters, and the Arts," *Living Age* 321, no. 4171 (1924): 1161.

32 Buster Keaton, *Cops* and *One Week*, VHS, (1920; Video Images, 1987).

33 Historian Cecilia Tichi has argued that the machine age emphasis on controlling efficiency was so pervasive that it gave birth to the concise poetry of Ezra Pound and William Carlos Williams and the tight prose of Ernest Hemingway. See Cecelia Tichi, *Shifting Gears: Technology, Literature, and Culture in Modernist America* (Chapel Hill: University of North Carolina Press, 1987).

34 Murphy Bed Company, "The History of the Murphy Bed," http://www.murphybedcompany.com/home.php?section=history (accessed March 1, 2007).

35 Earl H. Tate. Combination Furniture Structure. US Patent 1,122,170, filed June 8, 1912, issued on December 22, 1914.

36 Ibid.

37 Pasquale L. Cimini. Revolving Platform for Apartment Furniture. US Patent 1,278,108, filed December 12, 1916, issued on September 10, 1918.

38 "Germans Construct a Revolving House," *Los Angeles Times*, June 29, 1924, D9.

39 "Fact and Comment," *Youth's Companion* 98, no. 38 (1924): 616.

40 "A Revolving House for Jeweler Reiman: To be Built on a Turntable and Operated by Pressing Electric Buttons," *New York Times*, July 7, 1908, 3.

41 "Odd House that Follows the Sun," *New York Times*, May 22, 1927, XX8.

42 Thomas Parke Hughes, *Human-Built World: How to Think About Technology and Culture* (Chicago: University of Chicago Press, 2004), 29.

43 Angelo Invernizzi, quoted in Valeria Farinati, "The Sunflower Followed the Sun," in *Villa Girasole: The Story* (Mendrisio, Switzerland: Mendrisio Academy Press, 2006), 36.

44 Lidia Invernizzi, in discussion with the author, September 2006.

45 David J. Lewis, Marc Tsurumaki, and Paul Lewis, "Invernizzi's Exquisite Corpse. The Villa Girasole: An Architecture of Surrationalism," in *Surrealism and Architecture*, ed. Thomas Mical, 160 (New York: Routledge, 2004).

46 Lidia Invernizzi, in discussion with the author, September, 2006.

47 Lucia Bisi, "The Rotary Home: Villa 'Il Girasole' At Marcellise, Verona, 1935," *Lotus International* 40 (1984): 112–28.

48 Lewis et al., "Invernizzi's Exquisite Corpse," 164.

49 Lidia Invernizzi, in discussion with the author, September 2006. According to Lidia Invernizzi, her parents were not sun-worshippers like Dr. Philip Lovell, the Los Angeles naturopath that commissioned Richard Neutra and R. M. Schindler to design modernist houses that accommodated his healthy lifestyle and penchant for nude sunbathing.

50 Thomas F. Gaynor. Rotary Building. US Patent 895,176, filed on November 8, 1904, and issued August 4, 1908.

51 Michael Immerso, *Coney Island: The People's Playground* (New Brunswick, NJ: Rutgers University Press, 2002), 82.

52 Ibid.

53 The saga of the Globe Tower was reported throughout 1906 and 1907 in the *New York Times*. See "To Build 700-Foot Tower at Coney Island with Roof Garden Theatre at a Great Height," *New York Times*, January 21, 1906, 12. "Coney Island Reserves Out: Police Get Into Quarrel Between Tilyou and New Tower Company," *New York Times*, March 1, 1907. "Steel for the Big Tower," *New York Times*, April 9, 1907, 14. "Henry Clay Wade Arrested," *New York Times*, April 26, 1907, 1.

54 Laura Ingalls Wilder, Almanzo Wilder, and Roger Lea MacBride, *West From Home: Letters of Laura Ingalls Wilder, San Francisco, 1915* (New York: Harper Collins, 1995), 36.

55 "Aeroscope Attraction at Panama Exposition Like Enormous Inverted Pendulum," *Washington Post*, April 4, 1915, MS4 (originally published in *Popular Mechanics*).

56 Harlan Miller, "Over the Coffee," *Washington Post*, July 16, 1940, X2.

57 "Night Club Notes," *New York Times*, July 6, 1935, 16.

58 Bel Geddes, *Horizons*, 194.

59 Ibid.

60 Ibid.

CHAPTER THREE

1 D. Bruce Johnston, "The Use of Turntables in Buildings," *Architectural Record*, September 1965, 236.

2 "'Rotating' Garages Provide Maximum Parking Space on a Small City Plot," *Architectural Record*, October 1955, 247.

3 "The Met's Turntable," *Theater Design and Technology*, February 1971, 16. It was designed by theater architect Olaf Sööt and fabricated by Macton Corporation.

4 Norman Bel Geddes, "Flexible

Theatre," *Theatre Arts*, July 1948, 129.

5 Deblert Unruh and Dennis Christilles, "The Revolving Auditorium Theatre of Český Krumlov," *Theatre Design and Technology*, Winter 1997, 35.

6 Arnold Aronson, "Theaters of the Future," *Theatre Journal* 33, no. 4 (December 1981), 498.

7 Olaf Sööt, "Movable Structures for Stages," *Progressive Architecture*, September 1964, 197.

8 Anton A. Huurdeman, *The Worldwide History of Telecommunications* (New York: J. Wiley, 2003), 393.

9 Erwin Heinle and Fritz Leonhardt, *Towers: A Historical Survey* (London and Boston: Butterworth Architecture, 1989), 244.

10 Philip Hammon, correspondence with the author, June 12, 2007.

11 Harold Gulacsik and George Mansfield, *Space Needle USA* (Seattle: Craftsman Press, 1962), 9.

12 "Restaurant Perches Atop Building," *New York Times*, November 26, 1961, R1.

13 Charles H. Turner, "Hawaii Predicts Booming Summer," *New York Times*, May 29, 1960, X15. Construction of the Ala Moana Center came in the midst of a building boom in Hawaii, a response to the growing tourism market made possible by increasingly affordable and speedy air travel. In 1960 the new state had almost 250,000 visitors, a figure that was expected to double within five years. Between 1955 and 1965, the volume of construction work in Hawaii surpassed the amount undertaken in the entire previous century. See Lawrence E. Davies, "Hawaii Spurring a Building Boom," *New York Times*, June 20, 1965, R1.

14 Gulacsik and Mansfield, *Space Needle USA*, 16.

15 "Diners Reach a Turning Point," *Los Angeles Times*, December 3, 1961, 19.

16 John Portman, correspondence with the author, July 3, 2007.

17 Henry H. Lesesne, *A History of the University of South Carolina, 1940–2000* (Columbia: University of South Carolina Press, 2001), 186. The revolving restaurant was completed in 1967 using a turntable mechanism that was purportedly built for the 1964–65 New York World's Fair.

18 Such buildings were distinct from broadcast towers that were often built on high ground or on mountains (like the Seoul Tower in South Korea or the Telstra Tower in Canberra, Australia).

19 Mountaintop restaurants were on Zermatt, Davos, Lucerne, Brienz, St. Moritz, Pontresina, Grindelwald, and Les Diablerets. See "A New Swiss Peak in Alpine Dining," *New York Times*, January 11, 1970, 434.

20 *On Her Majesty's Secret Service*, VHS. Directed by Peter Hunt (1969; Farmington Hills, MI: CBS Fox Video, 1984).

21 Geoff Nicholson, "Done to a Turn At 360 Degrees," *New York Times*, July 13, 2003, TR21. These visits entranced Nicholson, who eventually became an aficionado of the revolving restaurant.

22 This arrangement also befitted restaurants whose location was overlooking a single, overwhelmingly important site. An example is the Merry-Go-Round restaurant in the Pushp Villa in Agra, India, adjacent to the Taj Mahal.

23 Jules Arbose, "London Landmark," *New York Times*, May 22, 1966, 485.

24 John Updike, *Roger's Version* (New York: Knopf, 1986), 312.

25 Robert Venturi, Denise Scott Brown, and Steven Izenour, *Learning from Las Vegas* (Cambridge, MA: MIT Press, 1972), 53. Quoted in Mark Gottdiener, *The Theming of America: American Dreams, Media Fantasies, and Themed Environments* (Boulder: Westview, 2001), 107.

26 *The Post Office Tower London* (Ipswich: W. S. Cowell, 1967), 29.

27 In the tenth century the Muslim theologian Abu Mansur wrote of a legendary city of dome-topped towers created at the behest of King Solomon. "Solomon sees rising from the bottom of the sea a pavilion, tent, tabernacle, or tower, vaulted like a dome, which is made of crystal and is beaten by the waves.…The aerial city is erected by the genii at the order of Solomon, who bids them build a city or palace of crystal a hundred thousand fathoms in extent and a thousand storys high, of solid foundations but with a dome airy and lighter than water; the whole to be transparent so that the light of the sun and the moon may penetrate its walls." Quoted in Rosemarie Haag Bletter, "The Interpretation of the Glass Dream—Expressionist Architecture and the History of the Crystal Metaphor," *Journal of the Society of Architectural Historians* XL, no. 1 (1981): 23.

28 One example from the 1930s was a scheme proposed in the magazine *American Weekly* that envisioned a six-mile-high tower with five steel conical platforms that would include "hospitals to give the poor the benefits of mountain climate," and "the world's greatest astronomical observatory in an oxygen tank at the tower's tip." See Lee Conrey, "Science Plans a New Tower of Babel Six Miles High," *American Weekly*, February 24, 1935.

29 Patricia Brooks, "Rotating View and Versatile Menu," *New York Times*, August 3, 1986, CN21.

30 Updike, *Roger's Version*, 328. The views were no better from the

revolving restaurant atop the water tower in Aachen, Germany. One visitor recalled it overlooking "large hills made from coal mining tailings, and a large teaching hospital that looks much like an oil refinery," http://web.cecs.pdx.edu/maier/france-report/report27.txt (accessed June 11, 2007). Scenes from an episode of the animated television series *The Simpsons* (1991) were set in a revolving restaurant that overlooked a prison riot and an individual contemplating suicide on a rooftop. "Principal Charming," Episode 27, *The Simpsons: The Complete Second Season*, DVD, (Beverly Hills, CA: Twentieth Century Fox Home Entertainment, 2002).

31 Quoted in James C. Cobb, *The Selling of the South: The Southern Crusade for Industrial Development 1936–1990*, 2nd ed. (Urbana: University of Illinois Press, 1993), 94.

32 See Michael T. Kaufman, "High Price of Prestige in Africa," *New York Times*, January 3, 1977, 2.

33 The Berlin Fernsehturm was not East Germany's first concrete TV Tower. The German Democratic Republic's first reinforced concrete television tower was completed in 1964. The head contained two cafes and an observation platform but no revolving restaurant.

34 When sunlight hits the raised patterns on these panels, it reflects the shape of a large cross on the side of the sphere, not the most desired symbol for the communist government.

35 Patrick Stacey, correspondence with the author, February 7, 2007.

36 Alexander Frater, "Travel: Off the Map: North Korea," *Observer*, January 1, 1996, 6. Another example of a recent prestige project with revolving restaurants was the Saddam Tower in Baghdad. It was built in 1995 after the first Gulf War. In 2003 the United States bombed the adjacent communications center, but avoided the tower so that it would not topple onto surrounding residential areas. See Marc Kusnetz et al, *Operation Iraqi Freedom* (Kansas City, MO: Andrews McMeel, 2003), 116.

37 Like its American counterpart, Macton Incorporated, Weizhong also manufacturers turntables for other uses. Vehicular turntables set in the floor of garages, driveways, and narrow urban lots are used to reverse direction and help automobiles and trucks navigate tight spaces. Since 2000 Weizhong has also produced display turntables used to provide a 360 degree view of new products such as cars and machinery at trade shows, expositions, and showrooms. Bing Xu, in discussion with the author, March 2007.

38 Ada Louise Huxtable, "Two Triumphant New Hotels for New York," *New York Times*, October 19, 1980, D33.

39 In the book *Food Tourism Around the World*, Tony Stevens asks, "Who wants to eat in a spinning restaurant? Why would you even think that would be popular, given the fact that moving while eating will at best give you indigestion and at worst probably make you very ill. Is it a gimmick to overcharge customers to consume some fairly average food? Or is it possible to justify the environmental impact of some of these restaurants— for example, the one which sits right beside Niagara Falls?" See Colin Michael Hall, *Food Tourism Around the World* (Burlington, MA: Elsevier, 2003), 9.

40 This comment, often mentioned in reference to particular towers with revolving restaurants, is derivative of an anecdote by the French writer Guy de Moupassant referring to the newly constructed Eiffel Tower. Moupassant regularly dined in the tower's restaurant to enjoy the city's only scenic vista that did not include the Eiffel Tower. Mentioned in Roland Barthes, *The Eiffel Tower, and Other Mythologies* (Berkeley: University of California Press, 1997), 3.

41 "City for Sale," *Nation*, October 2006. As one concerned citizen of Lahore, Pakistan, said, "We are offering swimming pools to those who do not have clean water to drink, glittering hotels with 500-ft high towers and revolving restaurants, while we spend long hours in the dark and over 50% of our people live in slum areas. Nobody is against development, but we seem to have our priorities all wrong."

42 Ronald B. Lieber, "Revolving Restaurants," *Fortune*, April 14, 1997, 32.

43 *Second City Television Network: Volume 4*, DVD (1982; Los Angeles: Shout Factory Theatre, 2005). The episode was nominated for an Emmy Award for outstanding writing.

CHAPTER FOUR

1 Arch Ward, "In the Wake of the News," *Chicago Daily Tribune*, November 23, 1944, 37.

2 Donald Hough, *The Camelephamoose* (New York: Duell, Sloan and Pearce, 1946), 26.

3 Ibid., 53.

4 *The Yellow Cab Man*, VHS, directed by Jack Donohue (1950; Burbank, CA: Warner Home Video, 1993).

5 Mike Weinstock, "Terrain Vague: Interactive Space and the Housescape," *Architectural Design* 75, no. 1 (2005): 48.

6 "For the Home: Tables that Revolve Serve Many Purposes," *New York Times*, September 15, 1951, 7.

7 *Ideal Home Exhibition 1968 at*

Olympia, London (1968; London: British Pathe Films). The show and revolving kitchen were visited by Queen Elizabeth II.

8 "The Playboy Town House—Posh Plans for Exciting Urban Living," *Playboy*, May 1962, 105.

9 Bill Osgerby, "The Bachelor Pad as Cultural Icon: Masculinity, Consumption and Interior Design in American Men's Magazines, 1930–65," *Journal of Design History* 18, no. 1, 108.

10 Lulu Fortune, e-mail message to author, November 13, 2006.

11 Alfred A. Granek. Rotatable Sections for Buildings. US Patent 2,823,425, filed December 16, 1954, and issued February 18, 1958.

12 Annette Müller (architect, Hanse Haus GmbH), in discussion with the author, September 2006.

13 Luigi Colani, in discussion with the author, September 2006.

14 Precedent for this anthropomorphization of architecture and urban design—the likening of architecture to the human form—can be traced from the writings of Roman architect Vitruvius to the designs of Renaissance artists and architects, like Francesco di Georgio's plan for a citadel shaped like a body.

15 Hanse Haus literature notes that the 20-by-20-foot layout in the interior would normally result in about 400 square feet of living space. However, in the Rotor Haus, the 194-square-foot living room actually functions as a 194-square-foot bathroom, 194-square-foot bedroom, and 194-square-foot kitchen. Add the 23 square feet of each turntable section and the 75 square foot toilet and closet space, and, according to the promotional material, the Rotor Haus essentially provides 680 square feet of total living space. Hanse Haus press release, undated.

16 Luigi Colani, in discussion with the author.

17 Clare Chapman, "In a Spin Over Rooms That Revolve," *Sunday Times*, October 17, 2004, Home Section, 4.

18 See Harold Krejei et al., *Friedrich Kiesler: Endless House 1947–1961* (Ostfildern-Ruit, Germany: Hatje Cantz, 2003).

19 Müller, in discussion with the author.

20 Colani, in discussion with the author.

21 Chad Randl, *A-Frame* (New York: Princeton Architectural Press, 2004), 41. See Chapter 2 for a discussion of postwar vacation-home construction.

22 William Butler, in discussion with the author, April 2007.

23 "This House on a Desert Revolves with the Sun," *Chicago Daily Tribune*, June 17, 1962, SW17.

24 Floyd D'Angelo (owner, Aluminum Skylight and Specialty), in discussion with the author, October, 28, 2005.

25 William Butler, "D'Angelo House," photocopy.

26 Roberto Lasagni, *Dizionario Biografico dei Parmigiani*, L'Istituzione Biblioteche del Comune di Parma website, http://biblioteche2.comune.parma.it/lasagni/gat-gio.htm (accessed October 8, 2007).

27 Bruno Ghirelli. Heliotropically Rotating Building Structure. US Patent 3,408,777, filed November 26, 1965, and issued November 5, 1968.

28 Harold Bartram, in discussion with the author, March 2005.

29 Phil Bridge (current owner of the Wilson house), in discussion with the author, May 2007.

30 Bob Thompson, ed., "It Turns Like a Giant Lazy Susan," in *Cabins and Vacation Houses* (Menlo Park, CA: Lane Magazine and Book Company, 1967), 47.

31 "This House Goes Around and Around and Around," *Mechanix Illustrated*, May 1964, 74.

32 The current owner of the Ford House has noted that the neighbors insisted that at least part of the yurt-like structure rotated at some time in the past, though drawings and the construction of the house prove otherwise. Sidney Robinson, in discussion with the author, December 2005.

33 Orson S. Fowler, *A Home for All; or, The Gravel Wall and Octagon Mode of Building* (New York: Fowler and Wells, 1856). Octagonal houses may permit less light to enter the interior as each room usually had only a single window and floor plans relegated closet spaces to the exterior walls.

34 Virginia McAlester and A. Lee McAlester, *A Field Guide to American Houses* (New York: Knopf, 1984), 235.

35 H. Ward Jandl et al., *Yesterday's Houses of Tomorrow: Innovative American Homes, 1850 to 1950* (Washington, DC: Preservation Press, 1991), 83, 84–91.

36 In fact, this rationalization and concentration of mechanicals and circulation in the center of the house was anticipated by Catharine Beecher and Harriet Beecher Stowe's 1869 treatise on efficiency and domestic science, *The American Woman's Home*. The book featured a design for a "Christian House" with rooms along the perimeter and a block in the center of the house incorporating a turning stairway, stove, shelves, a closet, and system for routing fresh air to individual Franklin stoves. Catharine Esther Beecher and Harriet Beecher Stowe, *The American Woman's Home: Or, Principles of Domestic Science; Being a Guide to the Formation and Maintenance of Economical, Healthful,*

Beautiful, and Christian Homes
(New York: Arno Press, 1971), 26.

37 Wernher von Braun, "Crossing the
Last Frontier," *Collier's*, 1952, 74.
The design was intended to serve
as an orbiting military base used for
surveillance and the delivery of
nuclear bombs.

38 De Witt Douglas Kilgore,
*Astrofuturism: Science, Race, and
Visions of Utopia in Space*
(Philadelphia: University of
Pennsylvania Press, 2003). Kilgore
defines astrofuturism as "an aesthetic,
scientific, and political movement that
sought the amelioration of racial
difference and social antagonisms
through the conquest of space," 157.

39 Oscar Dufau, Mark Zaslove,
Charles A. Nichols. *The Jetsons—The
Complete First Season*. DVD (Atlanta:
Turner Home Entertainment, 2004).
Some see the Jetsonian fantasy of
escaping to a life in the sky as a
metaphor for the era's "white flight"
depopulation of American cities. See
Lynn Spigel and Michael Curtin, *The
Revolution Wasn't Televised: Sixties
Television and Social Conflict* (New
York: Routledge, 1997), 47.

40 "Architect's Revolutionary Idea:
Living in a House That Rotates," *New
York Times*, September 3, 1968, 38.

41 Vivian Brown, "Round and Round
It Goes, But How is the Problem,"
Chicago Tribune, November 18,
1967, SA6.

42 Richard Foster, "The Circambulant
House—25 Years Later," unpublished
photocopy, ca. 1993.

43 Rolf Disch, in discussion with the
author, September 2006.

44 Down the road from Disch's
Heliotrop in Freiburg stand two other
projects by the architect that solidified
his reputation as a European leader in
green design, the Solarsiedlung (Solar
Settlement) and the Solarschiff (Solar

Ship). The Solarsiedlung is a fifty-unit
residential community that features
unostentatious modernist designs
but with triple glazed windows, a
system to recover heat from exhaust
air, and enormous solar panels on the
roofs. The Solarschiff is an adjacent
four-story commercial building that
includes offices, shops, and penthouse
residences. Like Heliotrop, photovoltaic panels and other energy-efficient
features make all of the residences
positive energy structures. These
designs were models of environmental
sustainability; in addition to their solar
attributes, all of Disch's buildings
relied upon local materials, suppliers,
and manufacturers.

45 Al Johnstone, in discussion with the
author, March 2007.

46 Ibid.

47 David E. Graham, "A Merry-
Go-Round Home," *San Diego
Union-Tribune*, March 6, 2001, B1.

48 As with the rotating houses seen in
satirical articles, books, and movies
in the past, the "smart house" of the
1990s has also been a source of interest
and ambivalence in popular culture.
See the 1999 Disney Channel film
Smart House, in which a high-tech
home malfunctions and has to be
overpowered by its residents.

49 Johnstone, in discussion with
the author.

50 Ibid.

51 Shiva Vencat (American distributor,
DomeSpace), in discussion with the
author, December 16, 2005.

52 Chris Wilson, "Join the Revolution," *Daily Telegraph*, October 9,
2004, Property Section, 1.

53 "Super Service! Hotel Changes the
Scenery," American Newsreel, 1956. In
collection of British Pathe, www.
britishpathe.com

54 Haigh Jamgochian, in discussion
with the author, April 2007.

55 Ibid.

56 "Rotating Apartments,"
Washington Post, June 17, 1965,
C8, 1965, 8.

57 Rolf Disch, "Heliotrop," undated
booklet, 30.

58 Rolf Disch, in discussion with the
author, September 2006.

59 Angela Tam, "A New Twist on an
Old Idea," *Asian Architect and
Contractor*, March 1992, 8.

60 Robert Ditcham, "Rotating Tower
to be Solar-powered," Gulfnews.com,
http://archive.gulfnews.com/
articles/06/11/30/10086170.html,
November 30, 2006 (accessed October
14, 2007).

61 Alex Frangos, "Dubai Puts a New
Spin on Skyscrapers; Planned 68-Story
Rotating Tower Part of Massive
Construction Spree" *Wall Street
Journal*, April 11, 2007, B1.

62 David Fisher, in conversation with
the author, October 12, 2007.

CONCLUSION

1 "A House That Rolls With the
Changes," *Architectural Record*,
April 2004, 75.

2 Lucille Davie, "Hillbrow Tower—
Symbol of Joburg" International
Marketing Council of South Africa
website, http://www.southafrica.info/
plan_trip/holiday/cities/
hillbrowtower.htm (accessed
January 4, 2008).

3 Sandra Mackey, *The Saudis: Inside
the Desert Kingdom* (New York:
W. W. Norton, 2002), 193.

4 Clarence Reed, in discussion with
the author, May 2007.

5 "Honour for Post Office Tower,"
http://news.bbc.co.uk/2/hi/uk_news/
england/2886617.stm (accessed
May 4, 2007).

IMAGE CREDITS

INDEX